# Inspired Work

*Showing Up & Shining Bright*

Erin Ramsey

*Inspired Work: Showing Up and Shining Bright*

No part of this publication may be reproduced in any form or by any means, including scanning, photocopying, or otherwise without prior written permission of the copyright holder or publisher except for brief passages in connection with a review.

Printed in the United States of America

General editing: Sierra Bower
Author photo by Krista Wedding, Grace James Photography
Cover design by Grace Winiger

Living Inspired, LLC

Copyright © 2017 Erin Ramsey
All rights reserved.

ISBN-13: 978-0998443829
ISBN-10: 0998443824

TO THE BRAVE ONES.

## ACKNOWLEDGMENTS

Kudos to all of you who are working hard while showing up and shining bright. You make the world a better place.

A wholehearted thank you to early childhood professionals and teachers who are helping to shape our future. You are valued and appreciated. Keep doing everything you can to show up and shine bright. Joy is shared not taught. Inspiration is contagious.

Thanks to Sierra, Grace and Krista for your incredible help and for shining bright. To Doug, Ryan, Sam, Luke, Jack, Molly, Isabelle and Anna, you inspire me to show up.

# CONTENTS

**Introduction**

**Operating Premises**

**Inspiration Baseline**

| | | |
|---|---|---|
| **Chapter 1** | Clarity of Purpose | 17 |
| **Chapter 2** | Heightened Self Awareness | 55 |
| **Chapter 3** | Affinity for Action | 99 |
| **Chapter 4** | Put People First | 135 |
| **Chapter 5** | Vibrant Energy | 167 |
| **Chapter 6** | Make Room for Possibilities | 199 |
| | **Conclusion** | 229 |

**Inspired:**

*of extraordinary quality, as if arising from some external creative impulse*

**Work:**

*activity involving mental or physical effort to achieve a purpose or result*

.

How old will you be in 5 years?_____

Your time is now to show up and shine bright.

# Introduction

If you don't remember the last time you felt inspired you are not alone. Most people are either working too hard or trying to avoid work. Many are often either stressed out or numbing out. The tools in this book will help you get back to your core, to your purpose, and offer new ways of working that will lift you and everyone around you up no matter what your job is! If you feel like you want a change, try attempting the opportunities in this book and you will discover doors opening for you. You will shine bright and begin to create a life of inspiration.

Work means: *effort done in order to achieve a purpose or result.* Work is our life; except for the limited time we may luckily engage in leisurely activities.

Inspiration means: *of extraordinary quality, as if arising from some external creative impulse*. To work with inspiration means that a good portion of your daily tasks are connected to your vision, aligned with your priorities, and your actions come from a place of joy in your heart.

When we make our work a reflection of our best self, quality arises. If we view our work as driven by external sources, it is likely that mediocrity and dread will start infiltrating our time and our effort. How many people do you know that get along well with almost everyone they meet? Who try their hardest? Who do their best every day? Who have big bold ideas and light up the room when they walk in? Probably not very many. This is your opportunity to be the one. Be the one that works with inspiration. Anyone can do it. You get to choose how you show up.

Life is more than waiting for Friday. You are intended for more than waiting for the workday to end, or waiting to win the lottery or hoping for the next big break. No more burning daylight watching your life pass by; the time is now to show up and shine bright for you and for the greater good.

Each chapter in this book is a choice you can make. Each choice has tangible tools you can use to act on your choices including action steps and affirmations to guide you. I am sure you will find that you already do many of the things outlined in this book. When you notice that you are; make sure you acknowledge what you are doing right. Build on your strengths. You can assess yourself on the Inspiration Baseline in the following pages. This can help you determine where you want to begin.

Most importantly, have fun while you challenge yourself. You can do hard things with joy.

## Inspired Work Operating Premises

We are intended to live joyously and abundantly.
It isn't what we do but how we do it that matters.
We are not what happens to us; we are how we respond to what happens.
We shouldn't use work as a scapegoat to our happiness.
We need each other.
When we shine bright we light the way for others.
There is more good than bad. What we focus on we get more of. Focus on love not fear.
Our lives are a reflection of our choices.
It is never too late to make different choices

# Inspiration Baseline

As you respond to the following statements think about the last month so you have a current view of where you are. Be honest with yourself. This tool is for you to determine where you want to put your energy going forward.

Circle where you are on each of these statements using this scale:

> 1=No/Never
> 4=Maybe/Sometimes
> 7=Yes/Always

I have a clear vision of my biggest dreams and greatest contributions. I know what I want for my life.

1   2   3   4   5   6   7

I am aware of how my thoughts influence what happens in my life and work.

1  2  3  4  5  6  7

I align my actions to how I want to be remembered.

1  2  3  4  5  6  7

I know what I stand for and I act with integrity.

1  2  3  4  5  6  7

I feel significant and know that I have impact on others in both negative and positive ways.

1  2  3  4  5  6  7

I know how to keep myself from getting depleted and I have many healthy activities that I enjoy.

1  2  3  4  5  6  7

I do many things well at work. I feel good about what I am contributing.

1  2  3  4  5  6  7

I carefully choose how I use my time because I know what my priorities are.

1  2  3  4  5  6  7

I know when I am ready for a new challenge.

1  2  3  4  5  6  7

I take action to challenge myself.

1   2   3   4   5   6   7

I am trustworthy, I don't gossip and I keep my word.

1   2   3   4   5   6   7

I have many people I trust.

1   2   3   4   5   6   7

I work well with others.  I get along with most people.

1   2   3   4   5   6   7

I am comfortable with open and honest communication.

1  2  3  4  5  6  7

I accept others easily.

1  2  3  4  5  6  7

I listen to others. I really want to understand them.

1  2  3  4  5  6  7

I look for and see the good in most situations and people. I believe there is more good than bad.

1  2  3  4  5  6  7

I feel joyful and have a high energy level most of the time.

1 2 3 4 5 6 7

I see beautiful things and experience beautiful moments almost every day.

1 2 3 4 5 6 7

I choose my responses to people and situations and rarely overreact or get angry.

1 2 3 4 5 6 7

When faced with a challenge, I look for solutions instead of complaining.

1 2 3 4 5 6 7

I actively look for ways I can help others.

1  2  3  4  5  6  7

I am often times curious.

1  2  3  4  5  6  7

I come up with new ideas.

1  2  3  4  5  6  7

I am always learning new things.

1  2  3  4  5  6  7

Add all of the numbers in each response for your score.

Total Score: _____    Date: _____

## Inspiration Baseline Score

175-125:  You are inspired in many ways and open to all of your gifts, talents, and possibilities.  Keep working to challenge yourself in areas you may have scored lower or in areas that you are most curious about. This is a good time in your life to create new challenges.

124-75:  You are ready to find new ways to shine bright and increase your contributions. You are doing some things to be inspired but should be looking for areas that will increase your positive energy and generate new possibilities.

74-25: You are ready to start a new path to break out of unhealthy thought patterns and situations.  You may be in a rut and looking for things to get you inspired. You are worthy and can do it!

Without judgment, think about where you are on the Inspiration Baseline. Now make a commitment to increase the baseline as you work through this book. Meet yourself where you are. Our lives go in cycles - this is an opportunity to create a positive cycle. You don't have to be perfect or inspired all of the time. The goal is to choose where you want to try new things, thought patterns and ways of working. All you have to do is make small changes and before you know it you will be creating a life of inspiration. Let's stop watching the clock and start living.

## Chapter One

# Clarity of Purpose

*Life is found in the dance between your deepest desire and your greatest fear.*
*~Tony Robbins*

In this chapter you will find the tools to help you create clarity through developing a big vision, managing your thought patterns, identifying what you want your legacy to be, writing your manifesto and answering the most important question of how you can serve.

Being inspired in life is essential in being inspired at work. I often wonder about the people who work with a spring in their step, who don't get sidetracked with drama and problems, who don't sabotage their contributions and who are able to rise above and soar higher when things get tough. These are the people who are inspired. I have discovered these types of people have clarity about themselves, their lives, their purpose and the direction they want to go.

When we are living without clarity we feel stressed out, like a hamster running nowhere. We feel the need to escape by creating unhealthy distractions from our lives. Things like watching too much television, zoning out on your phone, eating or drinking too much, or thinking and speaking negatively to ourselves and about others. We repeat mistakes, we burn up time and we feel depleted and worn out. Little things bother us and become big things because we don't have better things to focus on. If you have any of this as a part of your life, you are experiencing things like most other people. You don't have to live and work this way. You don't need to be like most other people. No matter what has happened, no matter where you are right now, you can begin a new way. That is your advantage; you have the chance to make choices.

This chapter offers you tools to help you get clarity. When we have clarity we are better able to make decisions, determine when we need to make changes, and know how to make time for what is most important to us. Even the smallest amount of clarity can be a catalyst to your brighter path. Small steps lead to big steps and before you know it the negative fades away.

The truth is most people spend more time planning a vacation or researching which car to buy than they do thinking about their life. As a result, many people are left wondering how they ended up in a life of stress and sadness. They start asking 'where did the time go?' Don't end up on your death bed wondering if you made your life the best it could be. Say good bye to being a victim of whatever ails your heart and get clarity about why you are really here.

Depending on where you are and what you are doing the clarity of purpose process can take days, months and even years. It is a process of unraveling the stories you have been told about how to live and how to be. It is a process of being courageous and accountable because once you get clear you can't blame anyone else for the things you might not like about your life.

On the same note, once you have clarity you will have so much more goodness come your way because you will be focusing on your best and highest self. The common and widespread drudgery and stress of work and life will begin to disappear. Use the tools. Make the time. Be brave. Clarity will create a better way of living and working for you. It will take effort; make this your work. Get creative; it can be your gateway to inspiration.

# Everything to Gain

*The secret of change is to focus all of your energy, not on fighting the old, but on building the new. ~Socrates*

Building the new requires a vision. A clear and bold vision for your life and your work brings inspiration. A big bold vision will create a platform for you to use your gifts and talents for your greatest contributions. The time is now to put your energy into what you want, shed the old and make room for the new. Time is passing no matter what you do, so why not live bolder and shine brighter?

One of the most life improving things you can do is expand your vision for your life and for your work. It might be scary or feel out of reach because, somewhere along the way, many of us have become afraid of disappointment, rejection, and failure. When we are operating out of fear we are limiting the possibilities for our life, and ultimately hindering the contributions we are here to make for others.

I am here to tell you that you have everything to gain and nothing to lose to begin creating a big, bold, fun and courageous vision for yourself. Don't let old thought patterns, fear, and doubt get in the way. You may be feeling defeated, unworthy or scared. It is alright, I did too.

In 2010, my life was a mess. From an outside perspective I probably looked like I was doing fine, but I was far from it. I didn't even realize it until I started getting sick. My marriage was falling apart, I was not the mother I wanted to be, and I was unhealthy and unhappy. I was sick of my job. I was negative, stressed, sick and broke. I was living in a quiet and unknown desperation for abundance and joy.

I started to create a vision for my life by writing down how I wanted my life to be. As I wrote my vision, it felt out of reach, outlandish, ridiculous and scary. While I felt hopeless, I also knew I didn't have much to lose to try to work on a new path.

I was apprehensive, but I also realized that even if it led to more disappointment as least I tried. I tried to create a mental rationale to be brave enough to dream a bit, and I suggest you consider doing the same. No matter where you are in your life or in your work, focusing on a vision will help. If you are down and out, give it your best effort. If you are feeling good, consider going bigger and bolder with your life.

I am optimistic that you can create inspiration in your work and your life. You just need to get started. Trust the process. Dream big. Break old, negative, depleting thought patterns. Take action. Be open.

Here are a few snippets of what I wrote in 2010. Keep in mind as you start your vision that as I was writing these words I felt it was all impossible. Everything in my life was completely opposite of these things. I was thinking it was utterly ridiculous and downright ludicrous, but today many of them are my reality.

*From Erin's Notebook:*
*12/7/2010*

*I present to audiences about living joyfully with integrity, compassion and courage all over the world.*

*I get to help people see their potential and understand their impact -I get to see beautiful countryside, meaningful historical landmarks, and enjoy exquisite food.*

*I have lots of friends who are genuine, loving, inspiring-who we can depend on each other, authentically enjoy each other's company and always have the best interest at heart.*

*I read a book every couple of days. I enjoy coffee, meditation and peace each morning. I have a bestselling book that helps people be their best and benefits those in their lives.*

*I am secure, confident and peaceful. I easily accept others. I laugh all of the time.*

*My children are healthy and happy. They enjoy spending time with Doug and I. Doug and I laugh together, support each other's interests and appreciate our relationship and our life of luxury together.*

All of this is true today. In fact, bigger and even better things have manifested in my life. For example, I did leave a long term job that I felt trapped in; and, I did stop spending time with people who didn't have my best interest. If we want change, we need to change ourselves and our environments and our influences in our lives. I did hit a lonely patch, but I reminded myself that if I wanted something different I was going to have to do something different. The things that have manifested on this list are the most important to me.

You might not know where to start, but these two tools from my book *Be Amazing: Tools for Living Inspired* are a great place to begin.

## Wouldn't it be great if...?

Answer this question over and over again. Write down your responses. They may start out with material things but as you press on you will discover your deepest desires. The trick to this tool is to focus on what you want and how you want your life to be - not what you want other people to do or have and not what you don't want. It is all about you!

Here are examples of what to do and what not to do:

Don't Do: *Wouldn't it be great if my co-workers stopped being snarky and lazy?*

Do: *Wouldn't it be great if I felt truly cared about and supported and made others feel the same at work? Wouldn't it be great if I helped everyone always put their best foot forward?*

Don't Do: *Wouldn't it be great if my boss wasn't so demanding and clueless?*

Do: *Wouldn't it be great if I communicated openly and honestly with my boss and we really listened to each other with the intent to understand?*

## Pick A Word

Pick a word to use as a guide for your spirit. This word will help you make decisions and stay focused on what you want. For example, my first word was 'peace'. This how I used my word:

If I have an option or decision to make I ask myself:

By doing this, will it bring more PEACE into my life?
Then my answers become easier and more focused on what I want. As well as, easier to say no to things I don't really want to do.

This is good way to determine what you do and how you do it particularly without guilt.

If I have to do things that aren't optional, like laundry, dishes, or paying bills, I use my word like this:
*I am going to do the laundry in a peaceful way. I am grateful to have a washer and dryer.*
*I am going to pay my bills peacefully. I am grateful to have some money.*

The fact is that all of the little things make up your life. How you do the little things creates how you live and feel. Choose your word based on what you want for your spirit. This word is not what you want for your children or friends or partners. It is for you to reconnect with you and make decisions that will serve what you want.

Once you have let your spirit be heard and your thoughts expand write down your ideas. Formulate your picture perfect life, at home, at work and in the community. Get yourself a nice journal, a good pen and a quiet space. Make this a fun, inspiring endeavor. It is really fun to dream big. Your life will start to change; and, when it does, make a point to notice the changes and express gratitude for them. If things aren't happening fast enough for you, stay patient.

If you feel a bit overwhelmed, try thinking of your ideal at work or at home first. It is alright to break it down and compartmentalize your vision by areas in your life as you begin to learn the process. It takes practice to let yourself dream big and think about the greatest possibilities for your life.

## Things to Remember When Creating a Vision

- ✓ Have fun.
- ✓ Be outlandish.
- ✓ If you feel nuts you are doing it right.
- ✓ If you are super excited or super nervous you are doing it right.
- ✓ Write it in the present tense.
- ✓ Focus on what you want; not what you don't want.
- ✓ Give yourself time; it takes practice to dream big.
- ✓ Use details. Day dream.
- ✓ Include where you will live, with whom, what you will be doing, how you are

feeling and what you have and what you give.

✓ When you are finished writing it, create a visual, often called a Vision Board or Dream Board. Frame it and treat it like a treasure. Put it where you will see it.

~~~~~~~~~~

## Action Step

*I make time to think about what I really want. I will write down what I want at work and at home. I will continually practice thinking boldly so I create space for the biggest dreams that are deep in my heart. I will discover dreams I don't even know I have.*

## Affirmation

*I am worthy of receiving abundance and living joyfully. My vision of my life and my work is big and bold. I dream big to help others do the same. My big vision and greatest contributions are my right and my responsibility. I have everything to gain.*

## Create New Thoughts Patterns

**What you think you become. What you feel, you attract. What you imagine, you create.**
**~Buddha**

It is common to put up mental barriers and thoughts to disrupt our vision. We may get scared, doubtful or return to negative habits in our thinking and in our actions.

Here are a few mantras/thought patterns you can use if you start to create mental blocks to your vision.

> I will be disappointed because none of what I dream about is possible.

***If the door doesn't open, it wasn't my door. No big deal there are plenty of doors waitng for me.***

> This is great for other people but not possible for me.

***I am worthy. I have great contributions to make.***

> It's all about working hard, not dreaming big.

***Big dreams create a beacon of light for effort.***

Nothing is happening. I am giving up.

*All in good time. Everything is unfolding just as it should.*
*I am keeping my eye on the prize and open to possibilities for myself and others.*

This feels greedy. I should be content with what I have.

*Having a big vision creates possibilities. I can be content and dream big.*
*The Universe wants to give me what I want. I am clearing the way while being grateful for what I do have.*

I just want to do my job, get a pay check and go home.

*I have influence everywhere I go and in everything I do. I will use my time to lift myself and others as high as possible. My work is much greater than any amount of money.*

I don't have the gumption and wear with all to achieve my greatest dreams. I never seem to follow through.

*It takes as much if not more effort to be negative as it does to be positive. I will think in positive ways about myself, my work and my life. Little things will make a big difference. I don't have to be perfect. I can trust the process.*

I am sick of trying and not getting anywhere.

*I don't have to be afraid of failure because I know when failure happens it means I am doing something that takes effort so I am successful regardless of the outcome. I might*

**as well dream bigger so I land in a higher place than if I had a small vision.**

I don't believe in all of this hocus-pocus.

**Vision jumpstarts you into action. It isn't magic, it is a catalyst.**

Why me? Other people deserve this more and there isn't enough for everyone.

**Everyone has different visions unfolding at different rates. I am opening my life to possibilities. I understand that if something isn't happening the way I wish it would that I have an opportunity to learn and grow from it as well be open to something even better. There is more than enough for everyone.**

If all of this good stuff happens other worse stuff might happen. The other shoe will fall.

***This isn't true. Life works in my favor. Good creates more good. I have what it takes to work through the hard stuff. Dreaming big is my right and my responsibility.***

Life has big plans for you. You just have to get out of your own way. Find ways to expand your mind and heart. When you expand your life you are truly serving others because you are showing them it is possible for them too. It may feel selfish at first, but it is actually the most unselfish thing you can do...light the way for others and have a lot fun for yourself!

I have seen this process work firsthand among my friends, family members and colleagues. Most of whom had many of the mental barriers listed above. When they kept thinking of their greatest life and practicing creating vision, their lives began to change for the better.  They were shocked but embraced the goodness and expanded their thoughts and beliefs even wider.  Even if you are a doubter or don't believe in it, or have given up hope, try these suggested activities and see what happens.

One of my friends was struggling at work with managing everything she needed to do and her team.  In her personal life, she left a twenty year plus relationship and was trying to figure out a new life.  Over the following years she had a lot of ups and downs but she kept trying to get a bigger and bolder vision for herself. She worked diligently on new thought patterns of giving up trying to control everything and began thinking in terms of possibilities After a long road she left an abusive partner, she revamped her work by simplifying, she moved and she is manifesting her dreams.  She sent a text to a group of us with an update that ended with, "I didn't like my life so I created a new one." If she hadn't been working on her vision of what she really wanted she may still be repeating and creating the same negative patterns of unhealthy relationships, stressful work and having a bogged down spirit. She did it. I did it. Lots of people I know have done it. You can too.

~~~~~~~~~~

*Action Step*

*I will pay careful attention to my thoughts. I will create new thought patterns to expand the possibilities for my life.*

*Affirmation*

*I am thinking big, believing big and being bold because I know when I shine bright I light the way for others.*

# Work Life Backwards

*Strive not be a success but rather to be of value. ~Albert Einstein*

A life altering exercise can be to work your life backwards. This reverse engineering helps offer clarity about what is most important to us and if we are aligning our thoughts, decisions and actions to what is most important. Many times we say one thing but do another; this is when our clarity is most compromised. Sometimes knowing what we don't want helps us realize what we do want. Thinking about your legacy, what you want to leave behind, can be a real wake up call.

When I decided to make changes in my life, I began to think about how my children may remember me if I was to die. At that point, they would have remembered a mom who was stressed out at work and at home, who was short tempered and distracted. I gave thought to what I would want them to remember. I wanted them to remember a mom who was joyful and funny and had fun with them. A mom who was encouraging and supportive and a mom who was a guide and not a dictator. When I got clear about the memories and the legacy I wanted to leave my children, I was able to make changes. I changed what I focused on, how I responded and where I put my energy. I even told them that I was going to do things differently. They help remind me, too! This is a powerful exercise and commitment. One day, several years later, I was out to lunch with one of my sons and we were talking about the changes. He said that all he remembers is "mean mom" and "nice mom". I would have been remembered as mean! I am so thankful that I became brave and honest and started aligning with my vision and my intended legacy. This might be your wakeup call; answer it.

*Think about your family. Think about your friends. Think about the people you work with and your neighbors.*

*Will your coworkers remember someone who was helpful and proactive or someone who complained and dreaded their job?*

*Will your neighbors say you were only concerned for yourself or that you were someone who was considerate and always willing to lend a helping hand?*

*Will your children and your partner remember a stressed out, distracted tyrant or someone who pulled the family together to have fun* and experience the true joys of love and trust and safety?

Imagine it is your last day on earth. How would you spend your time?

Imagine your funeral. What would people say about you ?

~~~~~~~~~

## Action Step

I will write down my best life eulogy. I will embrace myself and all of the gifts I have to offer others. I will shine bright.

## Affirmation

I align my actions, thoughts and decisions with how I want to be remembered. I am in a proactive state working towards the life I dream of even when it is hard and stressful.

## Make a Declaration

*Your beliefs become your thoughts,*
*Your thoughts become your words,*
*Your words become your actions,*
*Your actions become your habits,*
*Your habits become your values; your values become your destiny.*
*~Mahatma Gandhi*

After creating a big vision, developing positive thought patterns and identifying what you want your legacy to be you are ready to make a declaration. Making a statement and declaring how you want to be, how you want to live and what you want to work towards is a great way to hold yourself accountable by aligning your actions with your values.

Some of this may feel redundant or overwhelming. Please press on. Gaining clarity is a crucial part of showing up and shining bright so it requires effort and persistence. When we have clarity we are in touch with ourselves, prepared to act in proactive ways, the right relationships are developed, we have good energy and we get great ideas; a winning combination for inspired work!

This Declaration is a key piece to defining what you stand for, determining where to put your energy, and how you work and live. Your declaration is a concise, bold and true statement about who you are and what you believe.

Pick things that inspire you to write about and share them with the world. Declare your highest and best.

There are many ways to write a Declaration or manifesto. My suggestions are to begin with values, then beliefs and conclude with goals or actions.

Begin writing your declaration with some of these prompts:

My life and work are grounded in……

I believe in….

I will stand up for…

I will work towards…

I trust….

The answer is…

You can use any writing prompts, sentence structures, quotes, and thoughts you want. The key is that your declaration represents your core and the best of who you are and what you want.

Here are few of my Declarations to help give you an idea:

*I value all people, new experiences and the powerful connection to my intuition.*
*I know that joy and abundance are intended for me and others.*
*I will stand up for children, the elderly, women and the disenfranchised.*
*I will do my best to always work towards shining bright, because I know it helps others do the same.*
*I believe there is more good than bad in our world. I believe in the benefit of the doubt and expecting the best.*
*I promise to do hard things.*
*I believe the Universe conspires in my favor.*

*I believe in laughter and I look for beautiful
things and notice beautiful moments.
I will live big and take risks to grow.
I will always pursue how I may serve.
My greatest gift received is motherhood. My
greatest contribution is joy.
I believe in kindness and karma.
Love wins. Everyone is destined for greatness.*

~~~~~~~~~~

*Action Step*

*I will write my Declaration and share it with a
few people.*

*Affirmation*

*I take the time to know myself. I make the
investment of time in myself - it is more
important than taking time to buy a car or
plan a vacation. The time I take to declare
who I am has far greater returns for the quality*

*of my life. I know clarity is the first step in living and working with inspiration.*

## Purpose

**When you express your unique talents and use them in the service of humanity, you create abundance in your life and the lives of others.**
**~Deepak Chopra**

**How can you serve?**

Use your vision, your legacy and your declaration to concisely articulate how you can serve best. When we understand and embrace how we can serve we have clarity about our purpose. When we work with purpose we are inspired. Dig deep with this tool; it may take a while to get clarity.

Keep asking yourself how you can serve. Write down things that you do better than most. Write down things people tell you are good at and how you are helpful. Write down what you loved to do as a child. Think about what you do that moves time fast. Combine all of that with what you want and you should be able to write a sentence or two about your purpose. Clarity is key.

After lots of practice, persistence and courage my purpose is:

**To create joy with my energy and possibilities with my success.**

This purpose can be relevant at work, at home, and in the community. It is universal. It is a summing up of our spirit and gifts. True purpose is universal in your life. Take time to figure it out and articulate it. If it seems too daunting to determine your purpose in everything, start with work or home then build on it and see what crosses over to different areas of your life.

~~~~~~~~~

*Action Step*

*I will make time to think about and articulate my purpose through the lens of service.*

*Affirmation*

*I am clear on my purpose. I am brave and accountable for the gifts I have been granted.*

## Clarity of Purpose

## Highlights

- ✓ Creating a big vison for your life, at home and at work, will help expand your thoughts and actions.
- ✓ Managing your thought patterns will bring more abundance and joy into your life.
- ✓ Determining what you want your legacy to be will help you align your actions with your priorities.
- ✓ Declaring what you stand for will keep you accountable and inspired to take action to be true to yourself.
- ✓ Having clarity about your purpose will clear the way for service. Service is inspiring.

## Chapter Two

# Heightened Self Awareness

*You are built not to shrink down to less, but to blossom into more. To be more splendid. To be more extraordinary.*
~Oprah Winfrey

In this chapter you will find tools to help you become more self-aware through presence, enjoyment, managing your responses, and understanding what is holding you back so you can put your best foot forward.

It is not possible to give what you don't have. If I wanted to give you $5 and I didn't have $5 I couldn't give you $5. This is the same with everything in our lives. The way we can give to others is to give to ourselves first by considering our spirits. When we are cared for and peaceful, a door is opened for inspiration to walk in.

## Present of Presence

***Plenty of people miss their share of happiness, not because they never found it, but because they didn't stop to enjoy it.***
***~William Feather***

People who are high performing in their jobs and who are better connected to themselves and others are present. They are mindful of the moment. When we are present we learn faster, we listen to others better so less mistakes and misunderstandings occur, and we are aware of our own feelings and emotions so we are able to manage our responses in proactive ways. Presence helps us reduce wasted time and backtracking because of distractions.

The best gift you can give yourself is to learn how to be present. When we are present we are in touch with our spirits. The moment is all we have - we must stop fooling ourselves with distractions such as limiting thoughts and behaviors like stress, rushing because of a lack of time, and focusing on a scarcity of resources.

Learning to become present and to savor the moment requires you to think in new ways.

I feel like it is often a game I play with myself and my ego. My ego tells me that I have so much to do and there isn't enough time or people to help me. My ego tells me I need to pressure my children instead of listen to them. My spirit tells me the moment is now; embrace it, feel it, be in it and then let it go as the next moment comes.

We have put ourselves in quite a quandary telling ourselves that there isn't enough. Enough time, money, good people, whatever the story that you are telling yourself about not enough just isn't true. Everyone I know says they want to be happy. Most people keep retelling the distracted story how happiness is right in front of us when we become present.

Here are a few easy and fun ways that I teach and reteach myself to practice presence at home and at work:

## **Beautiful Moments**

Every day I intentionally look for beautiful moments. It can be anything: someone's smile, seeing people hug, watching a child laugh, listening to a bird sing, a ray of light coming in the window, enjoying a good song, petting my dogs, feeling my soft sheets as I lay down, warm towel out of the dryer...pretty much anything and everything can be a beautiful moment. They are all around us every day. It is in the noticing that they become beautiful. It is in the noticing that we become present. Share the beautiful moments with others or tell them when you see the beauty in them. Write down what you see and hear with your coworkers, friends and family. Change the conversations to beauty; make less space for the negative. Work will be more fun and home will be happier.

## Goodness Jar

On my kitchen table sits a big glass jar with a lid. Next to it are cute pieces of scrapbook paper and pens in a wire basket. When something good happens, big stuff and small stuff, I write it down and put it in the jar. Our goodness is on display. You can invite your family to write things down. There are no rules other than what you write is something you want to remember.

I took the Goodness Jar to the next level by gathering up lots of jars from second hand stores and gave them to everyone who wanted one that visited during the holiday season. Whoever took a jar committed to using it all year long; and, at the end of the year we will come back for a Goodness Brunch to share what is in the jars with the group. A fabulous celebration of goodness. It is fun to have other people doing it with you. You can do this at work and at home.

It is important, as you start to give yourself these little gifts and create new ways of thinking that you don't force it on others. It's important that you offer the opportunity to your friends, coworkers and family members without expectations because the Goodness Jar is for each of us to use in our own way if we choose.

Here is a beautiful moment that occurred without expectations. I was out of town and when I came home I was writing something down to put in the Jar. I noticed that all of the sheets of paper were stacked and folded together. Normally I just fold the paper in half and randomly put it in the jar. My heart was full thinking about someone in my family sitting at that table while I was gone reading all of the sheets of paper with beautiful moments and goodness abound! Don't you want your coworkers and loved ones to have the same opportunity? Give yourself a gift. Start a Goodness Jar for you first; then for others. The Goodness Jar will fit well on break room tables, reception areas, desks and of course in your home.

## Write it Down

I try not to make anything too much of a chore regarding presence because that would actually be counterproductive. I do offer myself the choice to write down things that I am compelled to remember; like a beautiful moment, a book I heard about, a quote I like, or an idea that comes to mind. This clears my mind so I can make room for presence.

How many times have you gone to the grocery store for two things? You repeated those two things in your mind the whole time while in store. You checked out, spent a bunch of money and didn't leave with those two things. If you would have written them down, chances are that you probably wouldn't have forgotten them and you subsequently would have created twenty minutes or so for a clear mind that may have had the potential to generate an idea, enjoy a beautiful moment or feel present.

I often think about how the average person doesn't generate any ideas or if they do they dismiss them immediately. I truly hope we can make a shift into possibility thinking instead of just to-do thinking. This is a good first step. It will serve you well. Don't make it a chore; look at this new practice as a gift to yourself.

*Tip*: I actually carry two notebooks; one for ideas and one for to dos. You can choose to keep notebooks in any way that you want. In the past, I divided one small notebook in half for each. Make sure the notebook and a pen are always with you so you don't waste time trying to find something to write with when a great idea comes to you.

## No Technology Practice

A few years ago, I was on the New York City subway when I looked around and I noticed that everybody was playing a popular game on their phones sitting and standing side by side but in total isolation. It was spooky and sort of sad. Games, social media, texting and emails often serve as distractions from the moment, the beauty, and the people around us. Look around at restaurants, public transportation, sporting events, elevators, hallways…pretty much everywhere we go people are looking down at their phones. Few of us are looking up and out.

We are missing opportunities for presence and connection. I started to realize this was a problem for me when I was seeing less beautiful moments and I was interacting less with my children and husband. I was getting less done at work and struggling to stay on task. I started creating practice sessions without technology.

In order to break a habit, you need to intentionally take action and practice. This practice can be implemented at work and at home. Here are a few ways to practice:

*If someone wants to talk and you are at your desk with your computer; move your screen and clear your line of vision to look at the person and listen.*

*If your work includes email, set certain times of the day to check it. When we keep checking email we are distracting ourselves from tasks and time to think. Set up email free work times. I often use a timer when I want to focus on a task, especially if the task is hard. While the timer runs I know I can only focus on the task, no email, no phone, and no social media; on the task only. It works out well; it is amazing how much you can get done when you regulate your distractions and impulses.*

*Set up times you can play games, watch television or look at social media and relax while you are not at work; just don't make it the whole evening!*

*I practice not having my phone while I go shopping with my daughter. I tell her what I am doing so she knows I want to be present for her.*

Be aware of technology and its lure. It is supposed to work for you. You aren't working for it. I still have my phone with me and I use it all of the time. Technology isn't going anywhere and it has many great things to offer. We just don't want to compromise our presence and our connection. Start practicing. Start talking about it. As soon as we acknowledge it, it loses power over us.

~~~~~~~~~~

*Action Step*

*I will look for beautiful moments. I will write down and talk about good things. I will make efforts to connect with others and limit my distractions.*

*Affirmation*

*I savor the present moment because I know that the moment is all we have. I embrace presence and grant myself the beautiful gift of being in the moment.*

# Be Your Own Coach

*Between stimulus and response there is space. In that space is our power to choose our response. In our response lies our growth and our freedom.*
*~Viktor E. Frankl*

The most successful and happy people have developed the ability to stop and pause in order to make space for themselves to think, reflect, and then respond to people and situations. Choosing your response is the highest level of awareness and enables us to embrace the most powerful thing we have at our fingertips: CHOICES.

    I like to think of myself as my own life coach. I can be aware of my feelings and thoughts and teach myself how to use them to my advantage so I am able to move in the direction that I want to go. I practice feeling what I am feeling. For example, if I am sad I let myself cry and feel the pain. Once I move through the 'big feelings' then I work on thoughts that will propel me. The same process goes for fear, anger, and judgment. All of the things that don't serve me.

I access myself as my own life coach without the big price tag. You can too. It takes diligent practice to know how to let yourself feel your own feelings then move on. Many times we get stuck in the things that don't serve us or we avoid them and bury them then they show up in unhealthy behaviors, feelings and interactions. So, walk the fine line and understand that it may take some time. It is quite exciting how we can teach ourselves how to respond in different ways. When you make this a priority, your life has less drama and negativity and your work will be more productive and efficient.

You can choose to create a big vision and make your best legacy a reality by approaching life in a proactive manner. Learning to respond instead of react automatically brings you to a place of abundance and influence.

Here are ways to be proactive versus reactive:

*Reactive*: Yelling or withdrawing when someone makes you angry.

*Proactive*: Thinking about why you are angry and then expressing yourself clearly and honestly.

*Reactive*: Jumping to conclusions.

*Proactive*: Asking questions.

*Reactive*: Making assumptions.

*Proactive*: Looking and thinking beyond your first thoughts and impressions about people and situations.

*Reactive*: Getting impatient or frustrated with others and situations.

*Proactive*: Use Mantras - learn to calmly choose your response. *All in good time. Everything is unfolding as it should.*

*Reactive*: Being judgmental.

*Proactive*: Remembering everyone has a story. Asking yourself how you can help.

*Reactive*: Going to self-doubt and negative self talk when you are scared or feel like a failure.

*Proactive*: Create new thought patterns. *I am learning just like everyone else. If I want more, then I have to do hard things. I am enough. I am worthy.*

*Reactive*: Complaining, being grumpy, exhausted and depleted.

*Proactive*: What small thing can I do for myself right now that will be considerate and loving? Practice sleeping when you are tired and eat when you are hungry.

*Reactive*: Feeling overwhelmed.

*Proactive*: Take a few minutes to breathe deeply and slowly. Get your thoughts in order, lower your shoulders from your neck and just think of your next step; not the next twenty.

Remember, a good coach will help redirect and pick you up when you are down. If you want to be a great coach to yourself, be accountable but also be kind. Treating yourself with compassion and being patient as you learn new ways of being and thinking will get you much further than kicking yourself while you are down.

Coaching yourself to a proactive mental state as much as possible will be life changing resulting in solutions being readily determined, ideas generated, arguments prevented and more energy for opportunities and inspiration!

~~~~~~~~~~

## Action Step

*I will practice becoming aware of when I have negative reactions and I will create new ways of responding. I will hone in on things that trigger me to be reactionary and will start practicing new ways of responding.*

## Affirmation

*I choose how I respond and react and I have the power to manage my moods and my thoughts. I know how I am feeling influences how I live my life. I choose where to put my focus.*

# Do Things You Enjoy

*Life is 10% what happens to you and 90% how you react to it.*
*~Charles R. Swindoll*

Life is meant to be enjoyed. Some of us get so caught up in what we have to do and what we have to be that we forget what we even like. Everywhere I go there are people who are disconnected from enjoying life. There are many reasons why so many people have become like hamsters running on a wheel going nowhere. I don't even want to begin to speculate about all of the whys and how's. Just know there is a better way to live that is waiting for you right on the other side of a few choices.

I use to be the hamster running nowhere and complaining, barking orders, feeling stressed, getting sick...spinning my wheels. Yes, I was busy but most of my lack of enjoyment was a result of my thoughts and responses. I know what it is like to work long hours, raise kids, be involved, budget, cook, all of things most people need to do. I also know that I have way more things going on in my life now with work, business, family, and friends; but, I am joyful, efficient and accept all of the good things that come my way because I know what I enjoy, what I want and that I am intended to live in abundance.

I use to think I couldn't enjoy life because I didn't have enough money, enough time or enough support. These were just thoughts. I created that reality. The good news is that you can create your own new reality by taking steps to enjoy life. Begin with small things. As you practice, big beautiful enjoyment will become a part of most of your days. The hard days will still arrive but they will depart way faster.

Here are some things I started doing to practice enjoying life:

>Meditated
>
>Walked
>
>Listened to music
>
>Prayed
>
>Grew friendships
>
>Played games
>
>Took baths
>
>Observed nature
>
>Slowed down
>
>Cut flowers
>
>Practiced gratitude
>
>Read books
>
>Watched funny videos

Think about what you can do right now to start bringing more enjoyment into your life. Try not to make excuses by blaming money, time or people.

~~~~~~~~~

*Action Step*

*I will do at least one thing a day that I enjoy. I will make it a priority and stay positive through the choices I make.*

*Affirmation*

*I am intended to live joyously and abundantly. I choose to enjoy my life.*

## Best Foot Forward

***Little things make big things happen.***
***~John Wooden***

My oldest brother said something to me while I was in high school that has stuck with me my whole life and certainly has served me well. I don't remember exactly what was happening but I think I was complaining about homework or getting down to the wire on an assignment and rushing and he said, "Erin, if your name is on it don't you think it should be the best you have? Your name means something."

Your name means something too. When we fully understand that we count, that we have influence and that we matter, we are inclined to put our best foot forward. When we put our best foot forward, even if no one notices, we are creating a new trajectory for our lives. The little things count.

If you aren't sure how to put your best foot forward on a daily basis a good prompt is to think about someone you admire and want to be like.

## Dress for Success

Putting effort into the way you appear is important because your appearance is a representation of you. Think about how you are, what you want people to think about you, and make sure you are projecting in ways that align with what you want. You might be thinking that appearance is just a superficial judgment - I think it is an opportunity for you to be understood.

If you want people to see you as you want to be seen, dress accordingly. Use it as a platform to put your best foot forward. In addition, I doubt you wrote in your legacy you want to be remembered as someone who rolled out of bed and into work. My guess is that you want to be remembered as someone who is put to together and enthusiastic to start the day.

A few things that should be known to all: wrinkled clothing, pajama pants, stains, and slippers are never a good idea at work no matter where you work. And you don't have to have a lot of money or expensive clothes and shoes to put your best foot forward. Just take care of what you have. Honor yourself.

Putting your best foot forward is really a gift you give yourself. Make a little effort in being intentional about how you enter the world.

## Be on Time

Punctuality in all things is a way to put your best foot forward. When people are chronically late it conveys that they think their time is more important than your time. When people are late for work it is unprofessional and inconsiderate and conveys the impression that they don't really care. If you are working on shining bright you should be doing things you care about. If you are in a situation at work you don't like practice putting your best foot forward and better things will come your way.

My mom always says, "I'd rather be an hour early than one minute late."

## Be Honest and Thorough

Pay attention to how you communicate and how you handle small details. If you make a mistake, admit it and look for a solution - don't try to hide it. When you are honest and thorough people will trust you more. Trust is the best platform for inspiration. If you have a small piece of paperwork or other item of minutia do it well. Practice. Make it count. You are building good habits that will bring you far.

~~~~~~~~~~

*Action Step*

*I will pay attention to how I am showing up in the world. I will take action to always put my best foot forward.*

*Affirmation*

*I matter. My name means something.*

# Stop Numbing Your Greatness

*From the beginning, the key to renewal has been casting off of old skin.*
*~Mark Nepo*

One of the most consistent things I see in workplaces and in families are people underestimating their impact. I believe there are three overarching reasons for this:

### 1. False Sense of Humility Driven by Guilt

For some of us, there is confusion between knowing you can influence people and situations and feeling arrogant. When we start to feel powerful, we realize that we can make change for the better, we can lift others up, we can share ideas and we can use our power for good. These are the fleeting moments of optimism, enthusiasm and inspiration.

Then, almost immediately, conditioned thought patterns interrupt our greatness with thoughts like these:

*I am here to get my paycheck and go home.*

*Nothing ever changes, why should I try?*

*These people don't understand and they never will.*

*Who do I think I am? I can't really do anything.*

*I don't want to look bossy or arrogant.*

*I don't want to be seen as the boss' pet.*

*I want my coworkers to like me.*

*I don't want to be disrespectful.*

*People don't listen to me.*

If any of these thoughts begin to take over your mind train yourself to go immediately back to your idea or action that made you feel powerful or influential or excited. You can make great contributions in small ways. Don't get caught up in the outcome; focus on the actions you are taking to free yourself up, limit your doubt and move into a place of influence.

Numbing our greatness is the fastest road to living a mediocre life and doing mundane/uninfluential work. When we show up and step up is when we are living as we are intended. When we do this with a kind heart and a clear vision of the benefits to others and ourselves, we are being completely unselfish and humble. True humility is service. There is no service in negative thoughts, poor habits and lack of action.

## 2. Lack of Awareness or Afraid of Our Personal Potential and Power

This is when we simply show up and hide or block out our greatness. When we are afraid of our greatness we often do the following:

*Watch too much television, play too many video games, or scroll social media.*
*Overindulge with food or alcohol or drugs.*
*Take a job that is too easy.*
*Don't finish things.*
*Make promises and don't keep them.*
*Repeat the same mistakes.*
*Hang out with people that don't inspire us.*
*Constantly act in a distracted state; not connecting with your children, friends, partners or coworkers.*

Here is the answer to all of the doubts, fears, and bad habits: It is your responsibility to unleash your greatness. It is your duty to shine bright.

Now, believe me when I say that I know that the things we do to numb our greatness can be daunting and feel unsurmountable. My suggestion is to start small. Here are few examples of small things you can do to break the numbing cycle:

*When I have an idea at work to make things better I will share it with at least one person who may be able to help.*

*When I get home from work I will drink water and get some fresh air before I turn on the television or computer.*

*I will pick one small task a day that I will finish well before I go to bed. It can be washing a load of laundry and drying, folding and putting it away instead of letting it sit in the dryer.*

*I will listen to the people in my life without distraction for ten minutes. I will put my phone away and really pay attention.*

If you start to do enough small yet intentional tasks your habits will improve and when your habits improve you will be working in alignment with your vision and priorities. I doubt that you wrote in your vision that you want to be unhealthy and disconnected from those you love, or that you wanted your work to be mediocre and your impact minimal. I am confident your intended legacy is not to keep a bunch of good ideas to yourself. It is necessary to break patterns to create new ones. No one wins when we numb our greatness. Everyone wins when we are aligning our actions with our priorities.

### 3. Feelings of Not Being Enough or Worthy

Feelings of worthiness are often buried deep in our spirits. It may take some reflection and thought about how you are living and what goodness you are willing accept into your life.

If this is something you might be interested in, I suggest *The Big Leap,* by Gay Hendricks, which explores this concept in depth. He refers to it as the Upper Limit Problem.

Signs you might need to work on accepting that you are worthy of all greatness:

*Tolerating people who don't have your best interest.*

*Making decisions based on fear.*

*Taking the easy way instead of pushing yourself to a new level.*

*Not protecting yourself from negativity.*

*Avoiding or sabotaging a promotion.*

*Pushing away awesome people.*

*Doubting yourself.*

*Being self depreciating and think great things for others but not yourself.*

*Only give to other people and not to yourself. Common ways this one appears in our lives are falling apart under garments, ratty bath towels, and messy purses. Making sure others we love have the best, but not giving ourselves the consideration we give others.*

To stop numbing your greatness can be quite complicated. If you think you need professional help you should seek it. But, there are small things you can do to begin unleashing your greatness. Start by being aware when you are afraid to step up and shine. Then, practice accepting and embracing your worthiness by taking action. The action can be expressing a feeling or thought, it can be doing something nice for yourself or deciding to do something healthier even if it is hard. Persistence and awareness will help you make big changes with small actions.

Everyone and everything has an impact; make you and your actions great.

You are destined for greatness.

~~~~~~~~~~

*Action Step*

*I actively look for ways to make things better at work and at home. I know I have impact and I make my impact positive by sharing ideas, working with integrity and shining bright.*

## Affirmation

*I am free of guilt and self-doubt. I have healthy routines and habits that serve as platforms for me to serve others, work toward my vision and align with my priorities.*

# Burn Up What No Longer Serves You

**Let go or be dragged. ~Zen Proverb**

Knowing what to stop doing is just as important as knowing what to start doing.

Hopefully you have made a commitment to start creating a bigger vision for your life. In order to move in that direction, think about things you can stop doing in order to make room for the new.

In the above tool, Stop Numbing Your Greatness, there are many topics that may not be serving you. Other popular things that get in the way of our best lives are: complaining, gossip, guilt, regret, negative self talk, fear, self-pity, victim mode, unhealthy habits, bad relationships, negative thoughts, snarky attitude, blaming others, feeling owed, grudges, judgment, distractions, rushing and stress.

When I first heard of releasing what no longer serves me I became a bit uncomfortable and started to put up mental barriers. I thought that it felt arrogant, overly deserving and entitled to only keep what serves me. Shouldn't I be serving others? The fact is that when we understand and embrace what serves us we begin to have more to offer others. If our lives are full of things that bog us down, that numb our greatness we are not serving anyone.

~~~~~~~~~~

## Action Step

*I will make a list of what no longer serves me and that I am willing to let go of. I will burn it or rip it up and say good bye to it. I am aware of the things inside myself that I let get in the way of being inspired. I choose to focus on what I want and how I can serve. I release the things that don't serve me.*

## Life Affirmation

*I embrace all that serves me because I know it will help me serve others.*

# Heightened Self Awareness

## Highlights

✓ Learning to be present will help you connect better to others and work productively and efficiently.

✓ Coaching yourself to be in a proactive state versus a reactive state will improve your life and increase opportunities for inspiration.

✓ Doing things you enjoy will make you feel better. When you feel better your life and your work will be more positive.

✓ Practicing putting your best foot forward will increase opportunities and convey what you want people to know about you.

✓ Figuring out what is holding you back and what no longer moves you in the direction you want to go will help you create a clear path for inspiration.

ERIN RAMSEY

## Chapter Three

# **Affinity for Action**

*You are what you do, not what you say you'll do.*

*~Carl Jung*

In this chapter you will find tools to help you overcome procrastination and doubt by taking action. You can develop routines and rituals, reflective questions and honing your vision to propel you and those around you.

## Be a Doer, Not a Talker

***Don't put off until tomorrow what you can do today. ~Benjamin Franklin***

Those who work with energy and purpose don't procrastinate. Procrastination is an energy drain and major distraction from productive, efficient work and it sabotages our inspiration. When we procrastinate we are putting our energy into worrying about what we need or should be doing. This uses up way more energy than if we just take care of business and move on. *Talking* about doing something and actually *doing* something are definitely two different things.

It is no fun to be the person who says they will do something, but when your colleagues or boss follow up with you, you have to say you haven't done it. You look bad for being unreliable and they feel frustrated because they were counting on you.

It feels great to follow through. Obviously there will be times when we can't do what we said we would. With clear communication, these times are easily remedied; however, if they happen all of the time they are not easily resolved. They actually define your character and your integrity to the job you are committed to do. Nobody feels inspired when people only talk and don't do.

It also feels great when the people around us are willing to pitch in, make things better and take action. If we have a challenge and come up with a solution but need help we are going to ask the doer not the talker. The talker points a lot, thinks their ideas are great but doesn't act on them, talks about how other people should be doing something and finding every reason why they shouldn't doesn't need to or can't do something. These types of behaviors limit possibilities, compromise trust and leave the talkers behind when bigger and better things are offered.

Being a doer is someone who pitches in, looks for ways to help, leverages resources to get the job done and generates ideas. To be a doer, one must be cognizant that which action they decide to take is proactive and aligned with priorities. It is a shame when doers are too reactive and spin their wheels because that just leads to frustrations and repeating of mistakes. The challenge is to balance doing with the next best steps; not the most obvious or fastest step.

If you lean towards being a talker, think about ways you can take action and pitch in. If you lean towards being a doer, check yourself and your priorities. When we use the best parts of talking and doing we create opportunity for inspiration.

Being a doer and not a talker will open more doors for you. People will go to you for help and for your opinion. They will respect you and trust you. It feels good when people count on us; when we feel good, we are more inspired.

*Doubt can only be removed by action.*
*~Goethe*

When we take action by trying new things we become more brave which makes us more confident. People who are more confident tend to be kinder and have more inspired thoughts and experiences at work and at home.

    I remember when I first thought about starting a business, I was so scared and even embarrassed to tell anyone except my husband. I was scared because I worried that I couldn't make it happen. I thought I may be delusional regarding my capabilities, and I was afraid of others judging me. I pushed through these feelings and mustered enough courage to have a meeting with a designer about a logo. It was the first step to creating a new inspired reality. I took action. I was doing. The more I did the more confident I became. This process happens every time I get ready to do something bold and new. The people who live their best lives are just like everyone else, but they push through. They act. They do. The process continues; we don't let ourselves get paralyzed by overthinking and only talking about things, we do things, we do hard things. You can too.

This same process happened when I set out to write my first book. I talked about it for years. The talking was masking all of the feelings and doubts listed above. Finally, one day I woke up and said I didn't want to be seventy years old still talking about writing a book. I would consider that a total failure; more than if I couldn't do the book or if it wasn't well received. Being a doer won over being a talker.

Don't wait till everything is perfect. Don't wait till you lose the weight, get the money, meet the right person or have the best idea. Act now; be a doer. Inspiration is waiting for the doers to show up.

~~~~~~~~~

## Action Step

*I will reflect on my behaviors at work regarding doing and talking. I will interrupt procrastinating thoughts and behaviors with action. I will look for opportunities to be a proactive doer.*

## Affirmation

*I am a doer. I act on my ideas. I actively look for ways to be a problem solver.*

Inspired Work

# **Routines and Rituals**

*When you discipline yourself, you're essentially training yourself to act in a specific way. Stay with this long enough and it becomes routine-in other words habit. So when you see people who look like 'disciplined' people, what you're really seeing is people who've trained a handful of habits into their lives. ~Gary Keller*

I really love this statement by Gary Keller, author of The One Thing, because when I struggle to achieve goals or get off track it is easy to be self doubtful and feel like a failure. Gary is saying that rituals, habits, and routines are what we need to be disciplined, not stronger willpower or to be less weak. We just need to build in what we want in our lives on a regular basis. It doesn't have to be a big struggle just a good plan that we follow through on.

Well thought out and enjoyable routines and rituals are what make you productive while you have fun, savor beauty, and shine bright. By proactively planning your day and being intentional about when you are going to do things and how you are going to do things, at home and at work, enable you to be proactive. Of course not all plans go as we expect, but for the most part routines and rituals are very useful in building good habits for proactively removing barriers and challenges.

There are two ends of the spectrum; those who do everything they can to do the least amount of work possible and those who only work. What we want to do is work toward the middle. Finding a good healthy spot in between is the best way to become a person of action.

My very favorite thing is waking up. I lie in my bed and the first thing I do is say, "thank you for another day". I love getting a cup of coffee, reading a morning devotional, planning my day and counting all that I am grateful for. I do this if I am tired, sad, happy or rested. It is a ritual. When I don't do it, everything is off kilter.

Here are ideas of things you can choose from for your rituals. Choose what will help you feel good to be alive, at home and at work:

## MORNING RITUALS

- Write down things you want to get accomplished.

- Think about the attitude and mood you want to maintain for yourself to be proactive and responsive to people and situations.

- Think about any challenges that may come your way and how you plan to handle them.

- Write down what you are grateful for.

- Make a plan to do the hardest thing first at home and at work; once you complete the hardest things for the day then you have freed yourself up for action and less distraction.

- Notice if your plans are aligned with your vision and purpose.

- Make your bed.

- Be intentional about what you are wearing and how you groom yourself to put your best foot forward.

- Go for a walk, meditate, pray, exercise.

- Drink water.

- Show love to your family.

- Enter your workplace with a smile and enthusiasm.

MIDDAY RITUALS

Check in with yourself during the day. Using the midway point is a good way to remember. This ritual can keep you on track with your morning intentions.

- Have you eaten and are you hydrated?

- Have you used the restroom (this may sound ridiculous but I meet many people who are so busy rushing around they forget or hold it; this is terrible for your health)

- Do you need a few deep breaths? Relax your neck and shoulders. Close your eyes and get present.

- Do you need to change course with your attitude and mood?

- Have you remembered the things you are grateful for?

## EVENING RITUALS

Think or write down:

- All of your contributions at work for the day.

- What you are grateful for.

- What you may have done differently.

- Talk positively to yourself. Stop all worry and negative self talk.

- Get your mind quiet; pray or meditate.

- Turn off the television and limit any negative information at least thirty minutes before going to bed.

- Drink a big glass of water.

- Sleep plans: Go to bed at a consistent time as much as possible. Try going to bed a bit earlier than you normally would. Many people are completely sleep deprived. It is hard to be inspired and productive when we are exhausted. Make sleep a priority. Be comfortable; pay attention to your sleep wear, sheets, temperature, sounds and smells. Create a sanctuary for yourself.

- Lay out your clothes for the next day so it saves time in the morning for you to put your best foot forward.

WORKPLACE RITUALS

- Assessing the environment for your comfort each morning. Is it organized, clean and comfortable?

- Managing your time with routines. Stepping back and thinking about new habits you can create with rituals that will improve your workplace.

- Make some time at the end of the day to prep for the next day. It can be a list, organizing and straightening up or managing your schedule. This helps get a good fresh start the next day.

As you think about what types of rituals you want to practice don't forget things you enjoy. Like my first cup of coffee in the morning or my silky soft pajamas in the evening. Incorporate little things you can enjoy and savor. One of my mentors had a lovely evening ritual of sitting in her sunroom doing her evening reading for work and/or pleasure. When she finished reading she would sit in her chair and eat one piece of her favorite chocolate. She would savor it in silence every night. This is so lovely to me because of its beautiful moderation and decadence. We need more rituals like this to create more inspiration.

Routines are a part of this tool because they help your day unfold without too much focus on the clock. Rituals are what you do. Routines are when you do them. Routines come first, what comes next, and next, and so on. If you have a little flexibility with time it is best to let your rituals flow. If you are always pressed for time then think about how you can incorporate rituals that will help you get in a relaxed, healthy state. Make a choice to use your time doing healthy rituals instead of worrying and rushing and being distracted. Remember, the most successful, inspired people are doing many, many things each day without being in a frenzy. They consider their actions as well as their wellbeing. You can too.

If you read this and wished you had more flexibility with your time, then put it in your vision. If you read this and thought 'I have no time,' like so many of my friends and how I use to be, I suggest you go to bed a bit earlier and rise a bit earlier. Even five minutes of intentional activity can create a better day and develop healthier habits.

~~~~~~~~~

*Action Step*

*I will make a plan to create healthy rituals in the morning, midday and in the evening. I will build on what I am already doing to care for myself and move in the direction of what I really want, at work and at home.*

*Affirmation*

*I navigate my life and my time in abundant, productive ways through rituals. My habits propel me toward the biggest vision for my life. I work well and live happily.*

## Progress not Perfection

***Continuous effort-not strength or intelligence - is the key to unlocking our potential. ~Winston Churchill***

We can **get good at** what we want. If we identify ways we want to improve our work then we can get a plan together and go for it. We don't have to hope, wait or dream about progress; we can make progress happen. We get to choose. Good doesn't mean perfect; getting good at something means getting better at it in a progressive manner. It is a process. Everything is a process.

I watched Roko Belic's documentary *Happy*. The main take away for me was that we can practice getting good at being happy just like we would do to get good at playing an instrument or a sport. Isn't this notion refreshing? It doesn't have to be a given that we are happy; it is ok if we have to work at it. We aren't flawed or unworthy or incapable. In fact, we are ahead of the game if we are putting effort into what we want. It is so simple, it is powerful: we can get good at what we want, even something as huge as happiness.

Happy people practice being happy; successful people practice what they are successful at. I practice what I want every day. I work to build my business. I take action to make space for new ideas. I let joy develop from the inside out. I am creating the life I want by getting good at what I want. The possibilities are endless.... we have choices where to put our effort. We just need to know what we would like to Get Good at. We need to take ACTION.

I am meeting myself where I am. I am remembering that it is not a flaw but rather an opportunity when I identify what I want to get good at. It is about exciting endeavors not judgment. It is an opportunity for action. This is not about success or failure; this is about embracing the process, being in the moment, focusing on what we want and living with a heightened awareness of our choices.

Don't fool yourself into thinking that the people you see who are happy, living awesome lives and appear to have everything they want aren't working to get good at how they are creating that type of life. They are choosing it. They are working for it. They are enjoying it. They are in process, just like everyone else.

What do you want to GET GOOD AT? What are you willing to take action for?

How can you be better at your job? What would you like to do differently at home?

~~~~~~~~~

*Action Step*

*I will pick something I want to get good at and will embrace the process of practicing and progression.*

*Affirmation*

*I am always learning and growing. I enjoy the process of progression.*

# Run TO Not Away

**Wherever you go there you are.**
**~Jon Kabat Zinn**

Setting yourself up to get in a proactive state of mind will ultimately shift the entire way you make decisions. An easy trap to fall into is trading one problem for another. We do this when we start to dislike something in our life so we find something else to do as a less unlikeable situation. It seems obvious but it is actually an insidious pattern that we need to be aware of if we want to live a life of great contribution.

Trading one problem for another often looks like this:

*Quitting smoking then eating more.*
*Leaving a bad marriage then starting a new bad relationship.*
*Resigning from a job just to start a new job that brings more problems.*
*Withdrawing from a friendship just to spend time with other friends that don't contribute to your happiness.*

There are times we need to leave, withdraw, resign and quit. In fact, we probably should do these things more often. BUT what we need to be careful of is running away from something instead of TO something.

How do you START <u>RUNNING TO</u> SOMETHING?

Get a clear vision of what you want. Refer back to the work you did in Chapter One: Clarity of Purpose.

Learn what your greatest contributions can be. Refer back to your legacy and your purpose.

Prepare for challenges.

Running TO something often looks like this:

*Quit smoking. Start exercising. Clear mind and healthy body.*

*Choosing to leave a bad marriage to find your power and strength. Once you find it, prince/princess charming comes along or you choose not to be in a relationship.*

*Reframe friendships or limit time with friends that aren't aligned with what you want. Friendships improve and space is made in your life for the right people.*

*Focus on what you want your job to be with the intention of service. Dream job offer comes. A door opens to bigger and better than you imagined.*

Stop shifting your life situations from mediocrity to mediocrity. Rather, go big. Dream. Take action.

Stay connected to the *Why:* your purpose. The trick is to do this during the most menial tasks. By the way, every single job on this planet has some aspect that is menial or irritating. It is a matter of where we put our energy. Are you going to stroke the flame of irritation and dread or you going to light your fire brighter by focusing on your purpose?

Our sense of purpose and our connectedness to our purpose can fluctuate depending on circumstances including our health, our relationships, our financial wellbeing, and our work. It is important to be patient with yourself while not letting yourself off the hook: even in the darkest days we can keep focus on our purpose to see us through.

I truly believe if more people would connect and focus with their purpose and their vision for their life they would make better decisions about who, how and what they do with their time, their future.

LOOK IN THE MIRROR and chart your course.

Work towards something. Move toward your biggest dreams. No more running away.

You have what you need inside of you; get out of your own way. Make a path for abundant and joyful living.

~~~~~~~~~~

## Action Step

*I will think about what I want and I will take action in that direction. When I come to a decision I will ask myself: I am running TO something or away from something with this choice?*

*Affirmation*

*I am clear on what I want. My decisions are based on what I want, not what I don't want.*

## Be Solution Oriented

**The most successful person makes a habit of doing what the failing person doesn't like to do. ~Thomas Edison**

It is not always easy to work in the direction of your dreams. It may get lonely to be the only one being a doer. The only one taking proactive action. It gets even lonelier if you are the only one focused on solutions and everyone around you wants to wallow, complain, be a victim, blame others, haphazardly do their duties, and speak negatively. No matter what, remember those that rise to their greatest calling and contributions, who operate from a place of inspiration are focused on solutions. Solutions propel you and everyone around you.

If you are trying to be positive at work it is really hard when the people around you are complaining and whining, try focusing on solutions rather than their behavior.

If things go wrong; look for ways to fix them. If it is out of your control; focus on what is in your control. Most of the time what goes wrong is your response and nothing else. If you aren't happy; look for things that will make you happy instead of focusing on what makes you unhappy.

*If you don't like it, change it. If you can't change it. change your attitude. ~Maya Angelou*

If your boss wants you to do something you don't like; ask yourself why you don't like it. If there is a better way to do the tasks or follow through on the request talk about it from a solution standpoint not from a resistant or complaining angle. Leaders like to work with people who have solutions.

Think about what action you can take to make the situation or challenge better. Make a list. Think about it.

Being solution oriented sets people apart. The rank and file is content with mediocrity and letting time pass. Those who are inspired enjoy looking for solutions. Embrace a challenge and know that problems come and go. Let yourself stand out; you are intended to shine bright and finding solutions is one of the best ways to do that.

~~~~~~~~~~

*Action Step*

*I will pay attention to how I respond to challenges and uncomfortable feelings. I will practice looking for solutions. I resist being stagnant and negative. I will grow and explore my options in all situations.*

*Affirmation*

*I am capable and willing to be solution oriented in all matters. I have control over myself and my responses. I make the choice to be abundant and proactive in my thinking.*

## Affinity for Action

### Highlights

- ✓ Being a doer instead of a talker will build your confidence and increase your energy to accomplish what you want.
- ✓ Creating routines and rituals will help you build good habits, be more productive and incorporate things you enjoy into your daily life.
- ✓ Choosing what you would like to get good at and embracing the process of progression will help you be action oriented and less judgmental of yourself.

- ✓ Making decisions based on what you want and not on what you don't want will propel you to inspiration and repel mediocrity.

ERIN RAMSEY

## Chapter Four

# **Put People First**

*If only you could sense how important you are to the lives of those you meet; how important you can be to people you may never even dream of. There is something of yourself that you leave at every meeting with another person. ~Fred Rogers*

In this chapter you will find tools to help you remember trust is most important, acceptance is a major human need, helping others and listening form lasting, powerful and inspiring relationships.

What are you leaving behind in your interactions and conversations? In the end, nothing matters more than the relationships we have formed, the influence we have had, and the love we have shared. If we know this, then we must take action to prioritize the most important things. We must choose our focus and our behaviors carefully. When we have trust, courageous communication and acceptance we create an environment where ideas and possibilities are welcome and expected. This is the type of place where inspiration thrives. A place we all dream of and a place we can all create. This is a goal of the inspired workplace. Inspired people inspire others. Inspired people influence situations and relationships for the benefit of everyone.

# Who is packing your parachute?

*We could put our lives in each other's hands without a second thought.*
*~Mr. Riecken*

I had a life changing lunch. The nonprofit I was the Executive Director of rented space in a half of a building. The other half was a shoe store. The landlord, the shoemaker and owner of the building, invited me to lunch. I didn't really want to go because I was busy. Little did I know that that lunch would be a gift of clarity.

We were going through a big organizational change at the non-profit. We had received a grant that was doubling the organization overnight. I had worked with several women for years building the organization with very little money but lots of experience and heart. My board was beginning to mandate higher levels of education as a result of this grant. In essence, wanting me to hire people with more education than my current team and let the new people have the higher paying jobs. I was devastated and frustrated because this success and funding was a direct result of the work my team had been doing for years.

I was in a fragile state and didn't have the experience to navigate both sides with grace. I was angry and I was sad, both of which don't serve well when it comes to being strategic.

I didn't know much about my landlord other than he was a shoemaker. At lunch we chatted and he told me about his hobby of building aircrafts in one of his warehouses. I was inspired by his 'secret' passion. I told him how my dad was an inventor. He was interesting and I was pleasantly intrigued and put at ease by him and his gentlemanly nature.

After an interesting conversation there was a pause. Then he asked me if there was anything he could help me with or anything I wanted to talk about. It was as if he opened a door that neither one of us knew I needed to be opened.

I told him about our big grant, about the board, and the staff. I told him I believed the board was wrong. While I understood the importance of high levels of education and that I would hire the new staff that had the requirements; I felt that the people who made this success happen should not be put on the back burner. I wanted them to be the leaders; they had the skills, the knowledge and the passion. Most importantly I trusted them. They deserved it. Yes, they should get on a professional development plan and go back to school, but they did the work and they deserved better than what the board was suggesting.

He quietly listened. Then he told me he was paratrooper in World War II. He told me that anyone of the guys he jumped with could have packed his parachute. He said, "We could put our lives in each other's hands without a second thought."

They trusted each other literally in life or death situations. All that really matters are the people you have in your life and if you can trust them. Who is packing your parachute?

My one-time lunch with a phenomenal World War II vet, shoemaker, and inventor has chiseled in my heart the importance of trust.

Trust doesn't just happen. We have to act in trustworthy ways. We have to expose ourselves to be vulnerable enough to trust another. The relationships and people you have in your life must be built upon trust. Nothing else really matters.

While the story went on with many wrongs, many rights and many lessons learned; I have never forgotten the importance of this lesson and I work diligently to never be put in that position again. In the position of working with people who didn't put trust above all else. And on another note, years later those women who built that nonprofit with me are still some of my closest friends. There is more to life than work.

We may never have to trust another with our life parachuting out of a plane into a war zone, but we do need to trust others with our hearts and minds in order to be inspired. Being inspired at work and home requires intentional effort to be trustworthy and build solid relationships of respect.

~~~~~~~~~~

*Action Step*

*I will look for ways to build trust with others. I will focus on building relationships with the people at work and at home with trust as the priority. I will be a person of trust.*

*Affirmation*

*I trust others and I am trustworthy.*

# Let People Be Who They Are

*As we learn to have compassion for ourselves, the circle of compassion for other-what and whom we can work with, and how becomes wider. ~Pema Chodron*

One of the most important human needs is to be accepted. When we are accepted we feel safe and understood. It is hard to refrain from judging if you haven't accepted yourself. If you find you have a lack of connection with others or if you have a hard time getting along and feel annoyed by others often think about how you may be feeling about yourself. Revisit your legacy, your vision and your purpose; this will help you to start thinking and feeling the way you want not letting stress, pettiness and reactions get in the way of connection with others.

When we feel accepted we can communicate, be who we are, and feel safe to share ideas and talk about challenges. This makes the best type of workplace regardless of the work and regardless of your position; you can start one person at a time. Begin to build trust, create a platform and things will improve.

You can't change anyone but yourself. When you accept yourself you can accept others with ease. Less time is wasted on judging and being annoyed. We don't always get to pick who we work with or who is in our family. We can pick how we interact and think about people who aren't a natural fit.

This tool I have learned through the school of hard knocks. I still need to practice this tool every day. It is so easy to project how you think others are or should be. Now if someone takes a different approach than me, I remember to let them be who they are. If someone wants something different than me; it's ok. I don't have to control them or the situation. I only have control over myself.

Letting people be who they are doesn't mean to overlook behaviors that are wrong, dishonest or unethical. You should and you must address those things. Letting people be who they are is accepting others in everyday life; helping them feel understood and seen. Look for the good.

~~~~~~~~~

*Action Step*

*I will identify when I am passing judgment or trying to change someone else.*

*Affirmation*

*I accept myself. I easily accept others. I have many healthy relationships.*

# I've Got Your Back!

**We rise when we lift others.**
**~Unknown**

It is the best feeling to be with people who have your back. The kind of 'have your back' that tells you they believe in you, that you can do it, and if you can't or don't they will be there for you. Are you someone who has your coworkers back?

It is easy to be that kind of person for those you love. The test is to be there for people you work with, especially those that it takes effort to get along with. This builds trust and trust is a platform for inspiration.

'I've Got Your Back' doesn't mean you will cover up unethical things or enable others on the low road. It doesn't mean hiding stuff from the boss, or covering up tardiness or doing things that aren't supposed to be done. 'I've Got Your Back' is for times when people are stretching themselves, doing hard things, being brave and need support. It is for telling people what they are doing right, pointing out their goodness, their effort and their beauty.

'I've Got Your Back' started a long time ago with a colleague of mine. She was retired and on her second career. She was probably thirty-five years older than me. I was her boss but she was a leader in many ways within the organization. I was young and had to fund raise and do presentations for big business people (which was scary at the time). I had one dress that I still have in my closet that I would wear. If I wore it, she would say, 'Oh, where are you going today? You have your 'money dress' on!" We would giggle; I would tell her what I had to do. This happened every time, and yes I had to get more money dresses as time went on, I would be leaving the office and she would say, "Hey Boss Lady, I've got your back!"

It was the best feeling in the world. It was an acknowledgement of me doing something hard. It was a support in case things didn't go my way. It was a kind gesture to say I believe in you.

Be the one who has someone else's back. See the good, point out the potential; focus on the possibilities because when we believe in each other we soar.

~~~~~~~~~~

## Action Step

*I will look for ways to support and encourage others just as they are. I will see when people are doing hard things and will tell them I have their back.*

## Affirmation

*I am the one that helps others soar. I am the one who has others' back. I actively share my encouragement.*

# Listen to Hear

*When you talk, you are only repeating what you already know. But if you listen, you may learn something new. ~Dalai Lama*

Listening is like presence; it is a grand gift you can give to yourself. When we listen to hear we are present, we are open hearted and open minded. When we hear we put our own thoughts, feelings and responses to the side; we show up for another. When we listen to hear we are compassionate and courageous. When we hear we put another before ourselves, we put people first.

As I travel and talk with people all over the world I consistently hear how rushed they are, how there isn't enough time. I can guarantee you if you are feeling rushed and stressed, then you are missing connections and opportunities to create solid, inspiring relationships.

People who are in the habit of rushing and being stressed have strategies they think work when trying to convey they are listening. They nod, sometimes at the wrong times. Try doing the "hmmhmm", sometimes appropriately but more often than not at random times. They are thinking of what they need to do next, checking their phone, looking at their computer or thinking about what they want to say. I promise you if you are doing this you are missing out.

It takes practice to slow down. It takes practice to listen to another person. It takes even more practice to hear the other person. These other people could be your colleagues, your partners, even your own children. Think back to your legacy, your vision, and your purpose. Does it say you are selfish and distracted or does it say you want healthy relationships with joy and real connectedness? Do you want to be remembered as dismissive or caring?

When we don't listen we cheat ourselves and sabotage our legacy, because your legacy isn't about social media or about if the laundry is done, or an email is answered or if a bill is paid. It is about how you show up for another.

Get present.

Use mantras to help you. "This is the moment." "Open Heart, open mind."
Put distractions aside. Physically remove them, shut a door, get a quiet space or let the person know you are listening. If you can't physically remove them; get a focal point on the person you want to listen to.
Open your mind and your heart. Let stress go.

Breathe.

Release your judgment, your fear, your own need to be heard and accepted.

Many times I leave conversations and the other person knows not a single thing about me. They may not have asked me a single question or inquired about my view or feelings. When I first started practicing listening to hear, I used to be hurt, sometimes annoyed and often felt lonely. Then I realized that I am giving what I want to receive and I am giving what other people need; a listening heart and soul. This is inspiring in and of itself. It feels good, it feels better to listen. When I need to be heard I have the right people in my life that will listen. This is created by giving. I try not to be the person that interrupts, talks louder than everyone else or dismisses people.

It has taken practice and continues to take practice, but life is better when we listen to hear.

My favorite thing about listening to hear is that I learn so much from other people. I learn about their interesting lives, their resilience to challenges that most people will never know about because they aren't listening. I learn about interesting hobbies, traditions, places to travel, food, feelings, and different points of view. When we learn from each other through listening we become inspired by others. We build momentum for our own inspiration. Sharing your ear is sharing your heart; we are inspired when we are sharing.

We are also inspired when we are learning and creating, listening does both. I learn how I can help. I create opportunities to connect the dots. I generate new ideas and many times new friendships are formed.

Slow yourself down. Clear your path for connection not distraction; inspiration will catch you.

~~~~~~~~~

*Action Step*

*I will intentionally practice listening to hear. I will identify times when I am distracted and compare the experience to times when I am not. I will develop strategies to be present and truly listen by setting my own thoughts and views to the side.*

*Affirmation*

*I connect with others. I have an open heart and an open mind. I help others feel understood and seen.*

# Courageous Communication

*Be brave enough to start a conversation that matters. ~Dau Voire*

So many times the problem really isn't the problem. Things get cloudy and confusing when communication isn't open and honest. I have been in many workplaces and have had so many conversations with people about their work where there is strife, stress, judgment, anger, and defensiveness. The majority of the time it all could be prevented with courageous communication.

Courageous communication challenges you to be open and honest. Courageous communication listens to the other. Courageous communication focuses on solutions and goals not defensiveness and internalization of false perceptions.

Aim for connectedness. The opposite of courageous communication is cowardly communication. Cowardly communication is gossip and negative self talk. It takes tremendous courage to nicely talk with someone about a problem, an annoyance, or hurt feeling because we are automatically in a vulnerable state. Many people don't realize when they become vulnerable and it will often lead to reactionary behavior. Complaining, judging, gossiping, and beating yourself up with negative thoughts.

We need each other. We need to feel connected and the only way to do that is through communication, even if we are afraid. Don't be cowardly. Cowardly behavior drains your energy and sucks any bit of inspiration out of your life and your work.

Don't let little things become big things.

You can be direct and nice at the same time.

You are only able to control what you do and how you do it; you can control for another person.

Courageous Communication includes:

- Expressing our true feelings without blame
- Asking questions
- Focusing on solutions and understanding
- Keeping the other persons' feelings and views with respect
- Not attacking
- Listening to hear
- Not taking it personal
- Being accountable

- Sharing ideas
- Admitting when we don't know the answer

Cowardly Communication includes:

- Deflection of frustration and defensiveness onto the what the other person is doing and saying
- Withdrawing and being a victim
- Making excuses for not being open and honest
- Gossiping
- Complaining
- Always having to be right

**Courageous vs. Cowardly**

Scenario: Something happens at work and you feel hurt and feel like withdrawing.

## Cowardly

*Your initial reaction is to withdraw, go home, and complain. Or you may walk down the hall and complain with someone who loves misery. You don't clarify or hope for solutions. You become the victim.*

## Courageous

*You stop and think about what is really happening. You approach the person, "I don't know exactly what happened or what you meant but I feel a little hurt. Can we just talk about it for a second so I don't carry it with me?" You keep the communication and responsibility for your feelings on your side of the fence. You provide an opportunity to clarify without attacking or withdrawing. This is courage.*

Scenario: You are frustrated because your co-worker isn't helping the way you think she should and the way you need her to. You are feeling angry because you are doing all of the work.

## Cowardly

*You tell your counterparts about it. You say things like, "She is lazy. She doesn't do anything to help." Or "I think she is dumb. She looks like a deer in the headlights and it is super annoying."*

## Courageous

*You notice these negative feelings and think about how to work to come up with solutions. You talk with your coworker to find out if she needs help or training. You ask for her help and share where you are struggling. You come up with answers together. If you need more help you talk with your supervisor but you don't go gossiping with your counterparts.*

Scenario: You are in a meeting and have a good idea about solving an issue.

Cowardly

*You wait till the meeting is over. You share your idea with a coworker that is your friend. You say things like, "I was going to say something but they won't do anything anyway." Or "I was going share my idea but the 'know it all big mouths' wouldn't't stop talking." You blame others for you not sharing. You don't take responsibility for yourself.*

## Courageous

*You feel a bit nervous and apprehensive to speak up among a lot of strong personalities. You ask to share an idea. You muster the courage. You are accountable to yourself. You know sharing was your responsibility; their response is out of your control. You feel good regardless of the outcome because you didn't blame or deflect.*

Scenario: Your boss asks you to do something differently to get better results. Your first reaction is feeling criticized and like she ever sees what you do right and she doesn't appreciate you.

## Cowardly

*You get angry and say something snarky under your breath. She ignores it. You get angrier and start complaining to your coworkers and your family.*

## Courageous

*You listen to her suggestion. If you feel criticized, you ask for clarification. "I am not sure why you want me to do this differently. Did I do something wrong?" You stay open for feedback and you listen to her perspective. You leave with a better understanding. You don't waste your energy; you stay proactive.*

~~~~~~~~~

### Action Step

*I will focus on being courageous in the ways I communicate especially when I feel hurt or apprehensive.*

## *Affirmation*

*I am courageous. I can be vulnerable by being honest and open. My focus is on solutions.*

## Put People First

## Highlights

- ✓ Building trust is key to all relationships and essential in inspired work.
- ✓ Accepting others and ourselves is the most important human need.
- ✓ Encouraging other people when they are brave builds inspiring relationships.
- ✓ Practicing listening is a gift to you and others.
- ✓ Using courageous communication propels you and the workplace to effectiveness.

## Chapter Five

# **Vibrant Energy**

*There are only two ways to live your life. One is as though nothing is a miracle. The other is a though everything is a miracle.*
*~Albert Einstein*

In this chapter you will find the tools to help you get on a joyful and free energy level by acting with integrity, approaching things with grace and ease, and being optimisitic and compassionate.

If you want to work with optimism and live with joy creating the right lens to see and interpret the world is of utmost importance. You can bring positive energy to all that you do with integrity, keeping your ego in check, and by giving.

# Take the High Road

*Whoever is careless with the truth in small matters cannot be trusted with important matters. ~Albert Einstein*

The best way to keep a high energy level is to do and think about things that align with your values. Actions and thoughts that assure your spirit are confirming that you are doing what is highest and best for yourself as well as everyone else.

When we do what is right we are operating with integrity. It begins with conscience effort. Anyone can develop this type of character even if you have compromised yourself in the past. Everyone makes mistakes, but having integrity is a choice.

Many people don't take time to identify and align with their values so their actions become contradictory to what they really want and how they want to be. This leads to a state of poor decision making and could manifest as laziness or inconsiderate behaviors and sometimes even unethical and illegal actions.

Taking the high road means you have integrity. You do the right thing. You know that small matters prepare you for big matters. You have a heightened awareness that your thoughts, feelings and actions have great influence on you and others. People who work and live with integrity practice self-reflection and revisit their course of action often to develop a seamless connection between their thoughts, actions and values.

Integrity is:

- Admitting mistakes and being accountable.
- Asking for help instead of worrying about how you look.
- Saying you are sorry.
- Doing your work to the best of your ability all of the time; not just when it is easy or convenient.
- Being authentic with your words and your thoughts.
- Never cheating.
- If a piece of clothing falls off the rack you pick it up.
- If you have a gum wrapper you put it in your pocket; you never litter.
- Never lying.
- Not gossiping.
- Stopping conversations that don't lift up others.
- Avoiding drama.

- Never talking poorly about someone else to feel better or look better or for any reason.
- Never taking a short cut that you wouldn't take if someone was watching.
- Treating everyone fairly and with respect; especially those that can't offer you anything.
- Giving credit where credit is due, no matter what.
- Being transparent with your actions and motives.
- Not trying to get something for free or ask for advantages if you don't really need them.

**The cream always rises to the top**. Often when we are acting with integrity and the people around us are not, our actions may be unnoticed: others may get ahead through lying and deceit. It can be frustrating to say the least. I have spent many days in my early career crying because people were doing sneaky, small yet deliberate unethical things that couldn't necessarily be proved or made right. I was devastated and frustrated. I could have easily stooped to their level. I kept on the course reminding myself to stay on the high road with humility, perseverance and character. Every time things worked out to my benefit; maybe not then, maybe not with those exact people, but things always worked out for me.

**Always stay on the high road.** Those who don't compromise the high road always will rise to the top. Preserve your character and your integrity at all costs. You will be well prepared and open to greater possibilities and opportunities. Never doubt doing the right thing. You win under all circumstances in the long run. The moment you compromise your integrity or lower yourself to the behaviors around you, you are on a lower energy level as well as a very slippery slope.

When I was twenty-eight I just started a big job as an Executive Director. I was on the phone with a board a member trying to learn how to cut and paste. Yes, cut and paste on a computer to complete a report that was due. As we were on the phone she started speaking poorly about the previous Executive Director. I was nervous because I just started the job and I needed her help, but I did not want to enter the position like this or to allow this behavior in my life. My knees were shaking. I was nervous, but I pushed through to what was right and said, "I don't want to be offensive but hearing about her isn't helping me do my job now." She quickly went back to the job at hand. I remember going home and telling my husband that this big opportunity might not be happening now since I said that. Even though we needed the money, he told me no matter what that I did the right thing.

This board member worked with me on and off for twelve years. She helped me through some difficult times in the organization and gave me pointers on how to navigate different personalities and perspectives. She was older than me and had experience and knowledge to share. I appreciated her help very much.

We never talked about that first phone call for all those years until my going away luncheon. She told the story of the phone conversation to the entire Board. She told them about the respect she had gained for me that day and how she appreciated me saying something. She told them that she would never forget it. Not everyone will respond as she did but we must do the right thing anyway. It really helps when you practice being courageous, know what you value and have people in your life that are supportive.

So even if you think taking the high road might compromise what you want remember the only thing that will compromise what you want is not taking it.

~~~~~~~~~~

*Action Step*

*I will intentionally reflect on all the ways I am interacting, talking, thinking, letting go, standing up for and willing to act on. I will make sure my actions and thoughts are seamlessly connected to my values.*

*Affirmation*

*I take the high road under all circumstances. I am a person of integrity.*

# Be Hard to Offend

*To offer no resistance to life is to be in a state of grace, ease and lightness. ~Eckhart Tolle*

If we are busy thinking about what 'so and so' did to us or what 'so and so' didn't do for us or what 'so and so' took credit for or what 'so and so' said, we are draining our energy. We are literally handing our joy and optimism over to 'so and so'. Stop wasting your energy on 'so and so' and start investing it in your vision, your values, your legacy and your purpose.

Being hard to offend doesn't mean letting people walk all over you or say abusive things to you. Being hard to offend means that you don't take everything personally. Most things that are occurring in other people are because of them, not you. Develop and set clear boundaries. You teach people how to treat you. If it is a regular occurrence that someone is taking advantage of you or not keeping your best interest in the forefront; it is time for new boundaries. What is happening, you are letting happen.

Here are some examples of when we get offended and sacrifice our grace, ease and lightness:
You get feedback or are encouraged to try something new at work and you take it as an attack or criticism.
*It is about the work, not you.*
You share an idea but it is not chosen to act on and you get hurt. Rather you choose to look at as an assault on your idea and yourself rather than there was a better option.
*It is about the idea, not you.*

There are many examples of when and how people waste their energy on being offended. Think about your own experiences. Are there times when you feel offended? Are you sacrificing your ease and grace complaining about what happened and how it happened? Step back and analyze your reactions. Step back and look at the whole picture.

Let's say you are at the convenience store and the cashier is taking a long time. You are worried you are going to be late for work. Do you get angry at her because she is making you late? Or do you step back and notice that she is in training and is getting flustered? You think about how hard it is to start a new job so you offer her a few words of encouragement as you check out. You may have even forgotten you were pressed for time. What type of person do you want to be; offended or graceful?

Even if you are certain someone is trying to offend you; you are the one who can choose to be offended. You can ask a question, you can ask them to stop, you can set a boundary but you don't have to be offended. You can use courageous communication.

I was on a conference call when a colleague told the group to just speak up and share their ideas or changes they may want to make to our proposed plan. She told them that we were hard to offend. She was right because we are about the work, the greater good and the contributions of all. We aren't about who had the best idea, whose idea got shot down, who is brighter, smarter or most clever. The latter is all ego; our ego tells us to be offended but when we take the high road and focus on things that bring good and vibrant energy we have no time to be offended. We only have time to set boundaries, and to work and act with integrity. We know others reactions are a reflection of them; our reactions are a reflection of ourselves. We can choose to respond with ease and grace. This is where real strength is developed and vibrant energy created.

~~~~~~~~~~

*Action Step*

*I will notice when I am feeling offended. I will step back and look at the whole situation. I will step back and ask myself if I am taking it personally. I will set boundaries; I will be responsive, not reactive. I will use courageous communication.*

*Affirmation*

*I am hard to offend. I live with my life grace and ease.*

# Expect the Best & Give the Benefit of the Doubt

*It is better to light a candle than to curse the darkness.*
*~Chinese Proverb*

We have more vibrant energy when we are optimistic and we try to see the best in people and situations.

What we see in others is what we see in ourselves. What we focus on we get more of.

To give people the benefit of the doubt doesn't mean to make excuses for them or ignore real challenges; it means you are mindful enough and proactive enough to consider causes, reasons and courageous communication when there are real issues to resolve. All of us have encountered at least one person who has taken advantage and has repeated the same infractions or negative behaviors; these are the type of people that we should help if we can, but shouldn't deplete our energy on.

We don't want to take the experience with one or two people who have depleted our openness and generalize that depletion to everyone else. For most people the benefit of the doubt applies. When we overgeneralize negative experiences we drain our energy and miss opportunities to develop relationships in an optimistic and open way.

Think about times when you made a mistake. A mistake that was truly a mistake but could have appeared self-serving, manipulative or undermining of someone else. You meant no harm or malice. Did someone give you the benefit of the doubt? Or did they overlook the other variables that contributed you to making the mistake? It may have been rushing, lack of experience, tiredness or misinformation or many other things. This is the same with everyone else.

To expect the best doesn't mean not to think critically and strategically. We should go into situations with our eye on the prize, thinking about the process and the outcome, and focusing on the best case scenario. There are always things to consider that may become challenges. These are important to think about, make a plan for, and discuss with others. The key is not to let them overpower the best case scenario for the outcome. This can apply to anything, a meeting, a dinner party, an interaction at work, and in our family dynamics, too. Focus on the best; expect the best.

When we expect the best we are breaking down our defense mechanisms that protect us from disappointment, fear of failure and rejections. When we give others the benefit of the doubt we are helping them break down their defense mechanisms of rejection, failure and disappointment. These two premises, expecting the best and giving the benefit of the doubt, are completely interchangeable in creating your higher level of energy for yourself and for others. Expecting the best and giving the benefit of the doubt is the fastest road to an open mind and an open heart.

~~~~~~~~~~

*Action Step*

*I will look for opportunities to expand my thinking to include the benefit of the doubt and expecting the best more often than not. I will treat each new encounter and new situation as a clean slate to open my mind and my heart.*

*Affirmation*

*I am open minded and open hearted. I am mindful and optimistic.*

# What will bring the most joy?

**True joy results when we become aware of our connectedness to everything.**
**~Paul Pearsail**

Joy is a choice.

Joy isn't knocking down your door but it is waiting for you to open it.

Joy can't be taught; it can only be shared.

Joy comes from the inside.

Can you think of anyone that you know who comes into a room and lights it up with their energy? A person with a feeling of refreshing, light hearted kindness that helps everyone feel and think a bit brighter. Maybe you are that person but if you aren't, you can be. You can choose what you bring into the room. We all know and can easily name those who enter a room and everything seems a bit dreary and darker. Let's try to create a larger pool of people who are lighting up rooms and people. It begins with you.

Conversations either create energy or deplete energy. Think about what you are talking about. Is it people and wrongdoing full of judgment? Is it ideas and possibilities? Are you complaining about traffic and the weather when you get to work? Or are you talking about a beautiful moment you experienced that morning? Are you talking about solutions or creating more challenges? Make your conversations less about what show you watched and more about something you are going to do. Be active. Be humorous. Be learning. Be accepting. Ask questions.

How you decide to spend your time also either creates or depletes energy. You can use joy as a guide in deciding how you spend your time. Much like using a word as your guide.

When making a decision about what to do ask yourself: 'What would bring me and those around me the most joy?" Think about joy at home and at work.

*Will watching trash TV or playing a board game with my children bring the most joy? Will zoning out on my phone or talking with my partner bring the most joy?*

*Will approaching a new assignment as an opportunity or a burden bring the most joy? Will expressing how I feel with courageous communication or burying my feelings with food or negative self talk bring the most joy?*

Sometimes joy feels like how exercise feels to a lot of us. Once we do it we are so glad; it is just busting through the mental blockades or bad habits and doing it. Do joy!

When you plan and develop routines and rituals use joy as your guide. Make sure you're inserting opportunities to create joy throughout your day. It can be having your most favorite uplifting song ready on your playlist when you get in the car to a beautiful mug for your coffee. It can be a full bear hug for a family member to fresh cut flowers on your desk. It could be a clean and organized workspace at the end of the day to your favorite pajamas. Remember the things you enjoy, the things that lighten up your mood and insert them throughout the day.

    Gratitude is the fastest way to create more joy in your life. A woman who attended one of my workshops created a 'Joy Door'. She put up a sign with 'Don't Postpone Joy. Find Joy Every Day' and each one of her family members puts something up on the door everyday. She told me that even if her kids were struggling to find something joyful they would talk it out and dig deep to write something down. When you focus on what you are grateful for you tend to focus less on the things that drain you. Build gratitude practices into your rituals. Create a Goodness Jar. Tell people what you admire or are grateful for in them. Write down what you are grateful for. Find at least one thing every day. You will have more vibrant energy and you will create more good in your life.

## Action Step

*I will assess my conversations, my routines and rituals, and my thought patterns for maximizing joy.*

## Affirmation

*I am joyful in all that I do and I think.*

# Be a Giver, Not a Taker

***The heart that gives, gathers.***
***~Tao Te Ching***

We enter life with the most important question: How can I serve? We look for ways to help, to contribute, to support and encourage. We are brave by sharing our gifts and talents and opening our hearts. We are vulnerable and we know it is worth it! We don't hide from our abundance.

Everyone wants to be happy. The way to happiness is generosity. A focus on others. A focus on your contributions. When you have a clear vision you can give to others. When you consider yourself and prioritize action you are giving. You automatically become happy when you give to others. This does not mean give until you have nothing to give. This means you give from a place of abundance. A place of joy and love. You enter places, conversations and situations with a lens of what you have to offer not what you are going to walk away with. This goes for even the jobs you don't love, the duties that are not rewarding but necessary. Those types of work are the true test of being inspired. Approaching situations at work and at home with the question, 'What am I going to get out of it?' immediately limits your vibrant energy.

If you want to be happy and feel valued; focus on giving.

If you want to be promoted and offered better opportunities; focus on giving.

If you want more doors to open and the right people to come into your life; start giving.

Being a giver is coming from a place of abundance. You create win-wins. You approach situations, decisions, and actions in a manner that makes sure there are no losers. Win-wins bring everyone to a positive energy level!

Being a giver creates a platform for the right people to show up. Givers attract givers. Takers attract takers disguised as givers.

Being a giver doesn't mean to be a doormat. A doormat lets people run all over them. A giver identifies what their greatest contributions are and shares them. A giver is open to receiving but doesn't act to receive. The giver's actions are aligned with her values, vision and legacy; not what she can get. When we align our actions with our values, vision and legacy, we will be given tenfold.

Remember actions are what makes us a giver or a taker; it is not who we are; it is our actions and actions can be changed.

*Examples:*

*Taker*: I will do a little bit more at work but are they going to pay me more?

*Giver*: I am glad to help out a little bit more; it will help everyone involved.

*Taker*: When I accept a job I only want to know when my vacation starts.

*Giver*: When I accept a new job I want to make sure it is a good fit with what I value and what they need. I do also make sure that the benefits are fair.

*Taker*: I will volunteer to bring food because I may need help one day and I want them to see me as a nice person.

*Giver*: I am happy to bring food to someone in need. I feel good and they will be served.

*Taker*: When I do something nice I always tell someone.

*Giver*: When I do something nice I like to keep quiet about it. I receive more than enough from the feeling of being kind; I don't need credit.

Imagine if everyone focused on being a giver; what a world we would have. Give yourself the gift of being a giver; opportunity is everywhere all day long.

~~~~~~~~~~

*Action Step*

*I will enter situations with a giving attitude and giving action.*

*Affirmation*
*I am a giver.*

# Vibrant Energy

## Highlights

- ✓ Acting and thinking with integrity keeps you on the high road; the road energizes you and limits energy drains.
- ✓ Approaching life with grace and ease leads to more connections and ideas instead of being offended and complaining.
- ✓ Being optimistic and compassionate leads to vibrant energy and better outcomes.
- ✓ Focusing on being a giver is the best way to live.

## Chapter Six

# Make Room for Possibilities

*Great minds discuss ideas.*
*Average minds discuss events.*
*Small minds discuss people.*
*~Eleanor Roosevelt*

In this chapter you will find the tools to help you listen to your intuition, ramp up your curiosity, and free yourself up to pursue your passion and take risks.

## Follow the Nudge

*The intuitive mind is a sacred gift and the rational mind is a faithful servant. We have created a society that honors the servant and has forgotten the gift.*
*~Albert Einstein*

We don't have to force everything we want. We don't have to plan to plan and worry to worry. When we are able to get in a proactive state of mind, learn to be present, and get quiet we are able to connect with others and connect with ourselves we are then able to feel and hear more deeply.

When was the last time you took action to learn about something or to think about something that peaked your interest? When was the last time you had a feeling or a little nudge in your stomach? Did you take action? A hunch? Feel a whisper to do something? Practicing listening to your intuition and noticing those gut feelings can help you be led to where you are destined to be.

I was meeting with a group of my friends; the POW WOWs. The POW WOWs are the power of women working on wonderful. I started this group because I wanted to have a platform with other women where we could talk about our dreams buried deep in our hearts, our fears and learn together as we grew together. I had friends but the platform wasn't there to really talk about ourselves as women, as people, as dreamers and doers. This POW WOW idea was a nudge I acted on even though I was a bit nervous. Now POW WOWs are popping up all over. If you are interested in learning more about starting your own POW WOW group, there is a guide in the *Be Amazing Workbook*.

At this particular POW WOW we were having brunch together. We were sharing our vision boards and celebrating the new year. We were talking about following the nudges in our hearts; listening to our intuition and letting it guide us. One POW WOW listened in awe and asked, "How do you even get a nudge?" This was a great question, a brave question because so many lives have become too loud with distractions, with unhealthy relationships, with limiting stories and overtaken with self-doubt that the intuition is drowned out. Her asking this question shows the power of the POW WOWS to ask the real questions, to be vulnerable and willing to learn.

Everyone discussed how someone can actually get a nudge. The answers included: trusting yourself, listening to your heart, goose bumps, a flutter of excitement in the stomach, a new thought that appears random, a person mentions something that you seem to hone in on, a new person enters your life with a unique piece of information or connection, a dream, a fleeting random thought, or a new idea that comes to you. The key is: we need to clear a path to receive them.

People tap into their intuition in lots of different ways - there is no right or wrong way. For me, I just started to notice little things and those times when I didn't pay attention to the nudge. For example, I was in the grocery store and I had a fleeting thought to buy a can of tuna. I almost did and then thought I didn't need it. The next day something came up where I did need it. Then I made the connection. It may sound silly to tap your intuition over a can of tuna; but, like anything else, building trust, getting quiet and taking action requires practice. As you begin to free these connections and act on the small nudges; the big nudges will guide you with certainty and clarity.

Our society teaches us to pay attention to the gut feeling when we feel danger or suspicion. Yes, most definitely. I also encourage you to pay attention to the gut for good things. Intuition is equally powerful in both good and bad because it is your power to unleash it. While you let it protect you from the bad also let the good guide you and protect you from an uninspired life.

Alignment with your nudges might at first appear as coincidences or a buildup of prior experiences. Your job is not to tear it apart or over analyze it. Just let you be who you are and let your intuition be the power that it is. Accept it as a precious gift. You don't need the one answer. All we need is the right path to lead us to the greatest possibilities.

The following tools in this chapter will help you avoid a frenzy of energy and practice with things that open up the possibilities. Being curious and experimenting and pursuing your passions are all avenues that will invite strong powerful nudges in to your life.

~~~~~~~~~~

*Action Step*

*I will slow down to listen and act on new ideas, feelings and situations. I will practice trusting my intuition in small things through practice.*

*Affirmation*

*My intuition is my guide.*

## Be Curious

**When you are curious you find lots of interesting things to do.
~Walt Disney**

Wonderment and asking questions can change you and the world. When we watch a young child we see wonderment and whys abound. They are trying to figure out how things work, pursuing things that catch their attention, having fun and learning. All of us were children: we still have that natural curiosity within us. Unfortunately, a lot like intuition, it has been buried and ignored. We have pushed aside the whys and the wonderment and traded them for stress and anxiety.

We have started answering the few questions we ask with the first answer that comes to mind so it isn't another thing on the to do list.  When we are rushing from one thing to another then going straight to numbing out, thinking we are relaxing we limit an opening for us to become curious.  Once again, if we can slow it down, get quiet, and practice presence we will create space to invite things that we want to learn more about to enter our lives.

Allowing space and presence to create the opening for wonderment and whys will open you up to unlimited possibilities. It is not difficult to create the space.  Here are few ways you can try:

*Get curious about others*: I love hearing people's stories. I love hearing about their experiences, their thoughts, and perspectives. Ask people questions. I know there is a fine line between being curious and just being nosy. I think our societal norms have limited us in learning about others in the name of being polite. Nosy is trying to get information to criticize, judge or gossip. Curiosity is for learning, creating a connection and offering a platform for another to be seen and heard. These are two very different things.

  I don't meet very many people who don't want to share about their experiences, their hobbies and share their knowledge. When we make connections like this it is so inspiring. My husband and I were at a farmer's market to do some market research for our lavender farm, Big Roots. We talked with florists, bee keepers, knife sharpeners, and tamale makers. Each person completely inspired us. We asked questions and they were happy to answer. We would not have had that type of energy or inspiration if we tried to be 'polite and not nosy'. Ask the questions. People won't answer if they don't want to.

Slow down your reactions by *asking questions about situations and decisions at work*. When we are in reactive mode we go straight to frustration, victimhood or lashing out. This happens often in the workplace with new decisions or challenging situations. Being curious can interrupt those reactive ways of operating. Rather than thinking, I told you so, this always happens, they don't care...why not think, I wonder why that decision was made? I wonder if I can do something to adjust? Do I need more information to fully understand?

Being curious instead of angry opens everything up to possibilities for learning, connection and growth.

*Look for more than one answer*: When we are rushed and acting like a hamster on wheel running nowhere, we want fast answers. We want easy answers that won't add one more thing to our frenzy. Some of this is out of survival - we can't stand around wondering what would happen if we didn't move when a car was coming at us, much like we wouldn't contemplate a tiger attacking us in the jungle. But these survival instincts and reactions don't have to be carried over into our entire lives. When we are surviving and reactionary we are just that: surviving, not thriving. So when you aren't in danger or trying to survive, open up your thoughts and options. Create alternative routes to solve a problem. Make fewer assumptions about others and ask questions. Get creative in your thinking. There is more than one right way...find as many as you can.

Being curious results in fewer misunderstandings, less assumptions, more clarity, less judgment, more acceptance, less speculation, and more ideas. Go beyond the initial curiosity and act on it.

Use these prompts to create a habit of curiosity:

*What else shall I consider?*
*Have you ever thought about...?*
*I wonder if...?*
*Why does...?*
*What would happen if...?*
*Wow, that is interesting...*
*I really like that....*
*That is so beautiful...*

*Action Step*

*I will create space to be curious. I will take action and pursue what I am curious about.*

*Affirmation*
*My curiosity leads me to my greatness.*

# Let's Experiment

**Doubt will kill more dreams than failure ever will. ~Suzy Kassen**

'Let's experiment' is one of my favorite mantras. 'Let's experiment' creates a path for courageous undertakings. 'Let's experiment' tells us that we can learn from failure. 'Let's experiment' conveys that if things don't go our way, or the outcome we anticipated doesn't come to fruition, it isn't a reflection of ourselves personally; it is an <u>experiment</u>, not <u>us</u>. The more often we can separate our ego from our action and ideas the freer we become to make room for possibilities.

Too many people are paralyzed with the fear to make a mistake or bad decision. How many times have you thought of an idea or pursuit you were interested in and told yourself, "it will never happen", "it's impossible", "I don't have what it takes" or "I don't have the resources I need"? What if you approached these situations with Let's Experiment?

My family and I have started a huge new adventure by selling our house in the city and buying a cattle farm that we have converted to a lavender farm. This adventure in possibilities will probably be my next book but in the meantime I will share that we have zero experience in farming. We made the decision fast - nudges bring certainty - so we are learning as we go. This is the best way to learn; we learn best by doing.

"Let's Experiment" has helped us in this endeavor. We made a pretty large investment in the initial plants. One day I was talking with my sons and they asked what we would do if all of the plants died. At first I had a moment of internal panic; but, I let it pass. I told my boys that I hope the plants don't die but this is our experiment year so either way we will know in the end. Then my husband chimes in with the notion that if not lavender then something better. With 'let's experiment' and 'this or something better' we were able to stay in the realm of possibilities, keep fear at bay and understand that failure doesn't paralyze us; we are driven by possibility. I tell this story because it illustrates that when we use our nudges and pursue our curiosity to do big things, we don't have to *start* with big things.

You can start practicing with small things. Here are a few examples that will help you put your toes in the water for making room for possibilities:

*You are drawn to a beautiful color and would like to paint a room with it. It isn't a typical color of grey, white or beige. You get nervous and doubtful. Then you tell yourself that you can experiment with this color and if you don't like it you can repaint it. Your room looks beautiful and you feel empowered to act on what you are drawn to.*

*You want to apply for the promotion but you are afraid you won't get it or if you do get it you might not be good at it. You tell yourself it is just an experiment so you apply. You get it and you love it. You followed your nudge to do something new and challenging.*

*You are sick of your drive home; you wonder if there is a more scenic way. You tell yourself it will take too long. Then you suggest to experiment with a new route. You love it. You see new things and you get new ideas. You might not take it every day but now it is there as an option for you.*

*You see someone with an awesome haircut. You wonder if it would look good on you. You worry you can't pull it off. Then you experiment knowing your hair will always grow back. You look and feel awesome; you trusted your taste.*

## Inspired Work

*You notice a beautiful flowering bush. You wonder what it is. You go home learn more about it and experiment with growing one yourself instead of saying you have a brown thumb or no time. This might even lead you to buying a farm.*

*You are sick of reading the same types of books. You walk in the bookstore and pick the first book that catches your eye. You decide to experiment so you buy it. You aren't caught up in the end result. It doesn't matter if you love it or not; you tried something new without spending hours deciding to try it.*

*You become curious instead of frustrated about someone at work that rubs you the wrong way. At first, you think it isn't worth it to ask about her anything then you remember you can experiment with relationships too.*

*You ask her a few questions and you find things you like about her. You understand her story a bit more. New connections are made because you experimented with an interaction.*

Little steps lead to great possibilities. Start practicing. Experiment! Free yourself up. Lighten up. Have fun.

Breaking old habits and thought patterns can help you open your life up. I was working with a woman who was retiring and moving to Florida with her husband. She was nervous to be changing her life and didn't know what to expect of retirement. This was a huge new beginning with huge opportunity for new possibilities, but she was limiting her thoughts.

Her new house was close to the beach. In our conversation I asked her if the first thing she was going to do was go to the beach. I envisioned her putting her feet in the water, feeling the sand in her toes and expressing gratitude for this new chapter in her life. She told me she wasn't sure when she was going to go to the beach. I asked her if she was moving to Florida to be close to the beach, thinking I was projecting my love of the beach onto her. She expressed her love of the beach and that the weather and the water were the reasons for them to be relocating. So I asked her why making a beeline to the beach wouldn't be the first thing she does when she arrives. She put her head down and said she would need to unpack and get organized first. I asked her why; those things will be there after she visits the beach. She told me she would feel too guilty going to the beach without unpacking and getting organized first. I suggested going to the beach first with gratitude might give her the energy and focus on the abundance that she was longing for and that would help her get the duties done in a more joyful energized manner. She had told me she wanted a more fun and positive life in Florida, this could be her first step. She needed to burn up the guilt and old thought patterns that were not serving her and experiment with a new way of living. She said she would experiment and try out going to the beach first. I never heard if she did, but in my heart I sure hope so.

If you are paralyzed with guilt, fear, habit or anything else that isn't serving you, this is your wake up call to start experimenting. You are intended to live joyously and abundantly.

~~~~~~~~~~

## Action Step

*The next time I get a thought, a feeling, or an idea I will experiment with it. I will follow the nudge and act on it. I will replace fear with experiments.*

Inspired Work

*Affirmation*

*I am free to explore all that life has to offer.*

# Pursue Your Passion

**The things you are passionate about are not random. They are your calling.**
**~Fabienne Fredrickson**

It takes a tremendous amount of courage to pursue your passion because passion brings powerful feelings and draws you into accountability for your pursuits. Put fear aside to discover your passions. Let yourself be accountable to what you are put here to do.

Use the following questions to begin the process of identifying what your passion are:

*What would you do if you weren't afraid?*

*What would you do if you won millions in the lottery?*

*Who do you admire and wish your life was more like theirs?*

*What are things you do that make time fly by?*

*What gets you fired up and angry?*

*What gets you excited and ready to take action?*

Make time to really reflect on your life and what you are passionate about. If you are at a loss to answer these questions know you are not alone. Don't throw in the towel. Pick one tool in the book and use it. If you start doing new things; new things will happen.

Eventually, your passion and vision align and your work and your life are inspired. Stay the course.

~~~~~~~~~~

*Action Step*

*I will intentionally look for ways to get in touch with my passion. I will hold myself accountable to my higher purposes.*

*Affirmation*

*My life is a reflection of what I care most about and my greatest contributions.*

# Keep Learning and Growing

*You weren't born to just pay bills and die.*
*~Unknown*

In order to make room for possibilities we need to embrace the notion that we can always be learning and growing. This is what inspiring people do. This is what good professionals do. If we believe we already know everything there is to know and have already tried everything there is to try we have completely closed the door to any possibilities that may be waiting for us.

## Inspired Work

At work, look for ways you can improve things, try something new and explore more possibilities. At home, do the same.

Here are ways you can keep learning and growing at work and at home:

Read new research and innovations
Read books
Have new conversations
Ask questions
Go to conferences on topics for work and on topics you are passionate about
Engage in art and music
Travel, even if it is being a tourist where you live
Meet new people
Notice things and learn about them

~~~~~~~~~

*Action Step*

*I will notice when I am stagnant in my thinking and in my actions. I will find things to learn about.*

*Affirmation*

*I am always growing and learning.*

# Room for Possibilities

**Highlights**

- ✓ Clearing the way to hear your intuition will guide you to possibilities and your greatest contributions.
- ✓ Practicing being curious and then acting on your curiosity will expand your thinking and your learning.
- ✓ Freeing yourself up to experiment will make life more fun and help you get in touch with your nudges.
- ✓ Identifying and pursuing your passions will lead to increased accountability and purpose.
- ✓ Being a life long learner leads to being inspired and professional.

ERIN RAMSEY

# Conclusion

## From My Heart to Yours

*Dear Friend,*

*Today is your day. It is your time to show up and shine bright.*

*You are more than enough.*
*You are destined for greatness.*
*You are worthy of all that your heart desires.*
*Your beauty, your energy, and your heart will never fail you.*
*You already have everything you need.*

*Remember always:*
> *You are intended to live joyously and abundantly.*

> *It isn't what you do but how you do it that matters.*

## Inspired Work

*You are not what happens to you; you are how you respond to what happens.*

*Don't use work as a scapegoat to your happiness.*

*We need each other.*
*When you shine bright you light the way for others.*

*There is more good than bad. What you focus on you will get more of. Focus on love not fear.*

*Your life is a reflection of your choices.*

*It is never too late to make different choices.*
*The moment is now.*

*With Love, Erin*

## ABOUT THE AUTHOR

Erin is an internationally sought after inspirational author and speaker. Erin has worked in the public sector for over twenty-five years in various leadership positions. She knows how to take ideas and put them into action and create teams that are inspiring and unique. She has a degree in child development and psychology as well as a master degree in public service administration.

She is the author of *Be Amazing: Tools for Living Inspired*, the *Be Amazing Workbook and Inspired Work: Showing Up & Shining Bright Workbook*. She has started a national movement to bring women together to share their dreams, fears and to learn together as they grow together. The platform is the POW WOWs, the power of women working on wonderful.

Erin resides in Kentucky where she and her family converted a cattle farm into a lavender farm. Their farm is called Big Roots and its purpose is to GROW PEACE. Big Roots is a place of rejuvenation and inspiration where day retreats with Erin are held. Visitors can cut their own lavender and flowers, walk the labyrinth and take in the beautiful countryside. Big Roots represents Erin's quest for living and working inspired!

To book Erin as a speaker for your event or to visit Big Roots you can email:

erin@erinramsey.com

To learn more about Erin's products and services you can visit: www.erinramsey.com

Grace, Luke, Sam, Ryan, Anna, Molly, Isabelle, Erin, Doug, Jack

*Photo by Krista Wedding, Grace James Photography*

ERIN RAMSEY

Made in the USA
Columbia, SC
03 September 2018